Living-Learning Communities in Practice

This book offers a roadmap for developing, growing, and sustaining living-learning communities (LLCs) that promote student success and enhance the undergraduate experience.

Drawing on the Best Practices Model presented in *Living-Learning Communities That Work*, as well as updated research and rich, real-life examples from LLC administrators, the authors offer a revised and improved model for effective LLC practice. Nuanced typologies guide stakeholders in developing and growing their own programs, from the foundational, to the intermediate, and to the advanced level. This text features an extended section on the assessment of LLCs, complete with a logic model for integrating program assessment with student learning outcomes, and concludes with lessons learned from the COVID-19 pandemic and a look into the future of LLCs in higher education.

At a time when colleges and universities struggle to create community for students, this book will be a valuable resource to practitioners, researchers, and institutional leaders to more effectively allocate resources to create and sustain LLCs and to realize the potential of these communities to improve undergraduate education.

Karen Kurotsuchi Inkelas is Professor in the Higher Education Program in the School of Education & Human Development at the University of Virginia, USA.

Mimi Benjamin is Professor in the Student Affairs in Higher Education Department at Indiana University of Pennsylvania, USA.

Jody E. Jessup-Anger is Professor and Chair of Educational Policy and Leadership at Marquette University, USA.

"This book provides an important update for best practices in living-learning communities. ACUHO-I is pleased to support resources like these that demonstrably improve the experiences of college and university students."

Association of College and University Housing Officers – International

"With their skillful re-envisioning of the Living-Learning Communities Best Practices Model, rich typologies for each model element, and illustrative examples from multiple campuses, Inkelas, Benjamin, and Jessup-Anger offer an indispensable roadmap for creating, assessing, and sustaining 'high-impact' living-learning experiences for students."

Jessie L. Moore, *Author of* Key Practices for Fostering Engaged Learning, *Director, Center for Engaged Learning, Elon University, USA.*

"*Living-Learning Communities in Practice* is essential for organizations that want to evaluate and improve the quality of their LLC programs. The authors revised the best practices model to reflect practitioner feedback and posed thought-provoking questions and practical suggestions for deepening quality."

Kirsten Kennedy, *Associate Vice President, The Residential Experience, University of South Carolina, USA.*

"In this edition of *Living-Learning Communities in Practice,* the authors have provided a valuable tool, pathway and guidebook for academics and practitioners alike. Their real-world approach to evolving previous thought processes is a testament to the ongoing importance of LLCs as a High Impact Practice."

Kathy Bush Hobgood, *Associate Vice-President for Auxiliary Enterprises, Clemson University, USA.*

Living-Learning Communities in Practice

A Guide for Creating, Maintaining, and Sustaining Effective Programs in Higher Education

Karen Kurotsuchi Inkelas,
Mimi Benjamin, and
Jody E. Jessup-Anger

Routledge
Taylor & Francis Group
NEW YORK AND LONDON

acuho-i

Designed cover image: Getty

First published 2024
by Routledge
605 Third Avenue, New York, NY 10158

and by Routledge
4 Park Square, Milton Park, Abingdon, Oxon, OX14 4RN

Routledge is an imprint of the Taylor & Francis Group, an informa business

© 2024 Taylor & Francis

The right of Karen Kurotsuchi Inkelas, Mimi Benjamin, and Jody E. Jessup-Anger to be identified as authors of this work has been asserted in accordance with sections 77 and 78 of the Copyright, Designs and Patents Act 1988.

All rights reserved. No part of this book may be reprinted or reproduced or utilised in any form or by any electronic, mechanical, or other means, now known or hereafter invented, including photocopying and recording, or in any information storage or retrieval system, without permission in writing from the publishers.

Trademark notice: Product or corporate names may be trademarks or registered trademarks, and are used only for identification and explanation without intent to infringe.

Library of Congress Cataloging-in-Publication Data
Names: Inkelas, Karen Kurotsuchi, author. | Benjamin, Mimi, author. | Jessup-Anger, Jody, 1975– author.
Title: Living-learning communities in practice: a guide for creating, maintaining, and sustaining effective programs in higher education / Karen Kurotsuchi Inkelas, Mimi Benjamin and Jody E. Jessup-Anger.
Description: New York, NY: Routledge, 2024. |
Includes bibliographical references and index. |
Identifiers: LCCN 2023054792 (print) | LCCN 2023054793 (ebook) | ISBN 9781642673210 (paperback) | ISBN 9781642673210 (hardback) | ISBN 9781003445784 (ebook)
Subjects: LCSH: Student learning communities. | Group work in education. | Active learning.
Classification: LCC LB1032 .I4924 2024 (print) | LCC LB1032 (ebook) | DDC 371.3—dc23/eng/20231214
LC record available at https://lccn.loc.gov/2023054792
LC ebook record available at https://lccn.loc.gov/2023054793

ISBN: 978-1-642-67320-3 (hbk)
ISBN: 978-1-642-67321-0 (pbk)
ISBN: 978-1-003-44578-4 (ebk)

DOI: 10.4324/9781003445784

Typeset in Perpetua
by codeMantra

To the Hereford Residential College community at the University of Virginia – my home and heart from 2018 to 2023 (Karen Kurotsuchi Inkelas)

To Mike Howland – my constant support; and to Denielle Gower – because I promised (Mimi Benjamin)

To my family – my joy and purpose; and to Mimi and Karen who make every project more fun and meaningful (Jody Jessup-Anger)

Contents

Foreword ix
  MarQuita Barker and Peter Felten
Acknowledgments xii

1 Introduction to Living-Learning Communities in Practice 1

2 The Revised Living-Learning Communities Best Practices Model 10

3 Best Practices in Living-Learning Communities: Infrastructure 17

4 Best Practices in Living-Learning Communities: Climate 40

5 Best Practices in Living-Learning Communities: Intellectual Experience 55

6 Best Practices in Living-Learning Communities: Social Experience 65

7 Best Practices in Living-Learning Communities: Student Outcomes Through Assessment 77

8 Best Practices in Living-Learning Communities: Integration and Communication 95

9 Final Thoughts on Living-Learning Communities in Practice   107

Afterword   *115*
  Jillian Kinzie
Index   *123*

Foreword

Location, location, location. Realtors repeat that mantra because where you live matters.

In higher education, however, research clearly shows that the location of where you live is <u>not</u> as important as *what you do where you live* (Mayhew et al., 2016). Our own experiences as college students illustrates this:

- MarQuita left home at age 17 to attend a large four-year public university. Although the school had over 30,000 undergraduates, she moved into a living-learning community (LLC) her first semester. This hall of 42 students taking English and Math together made it feel much smaller and much more digestible. To this day, she remembers the names and faces of her classmates in the LLC, the long nights studying together in the common lounges, and the informal support groups they were able to form due to their proximity – not only learning *with* each other but also *from* each other.
- Peter left home at age 17 to attend a mid-sized private university. Although his college had only one-fifth of the student population of MarQuita's, he moved into a dormitory tower that housed more than 700 first-year male students – nicknamed "the beer can" because that's what it looked, and smelled, like. He remembers long nights studying or relaxing with peers, but his academic and social community came from affiliations mostly outside the dorm. Today, he struggles to name even a handful of people who lived in his first-year dorm.

Our two stories, of course, are only anecdotes, but they underscore the importance of what institutions do – or don't do – to scaffold student learning and well-being in their residence halls.

In this book, authors Karen Kurotsuchi Inkelas, Mimi Benjamin, and Jody Jessup-Anger show us how LLCs at colleges and universities can create an environment that enables student success, well-being, and belonging. At a time when some are questioning the need for post-secondary education at all, this book doubles down on the idea that residential education done intentionally and purposefully can be transformational – and provides a research-based framework to support any institution in designing LLCs that work.

This text builds from the authors' 2018 book that introduced the Best Practices Model (BPM) for the design of LLCs. In this new and substantially revised volume, the authors make several significant changes to the BPM to account for the experiences and feedback of readers who work in or research LLCs. These revisions not only improve the model but also underscore the fundamental purpose of the model – to support the development and evolution of high-quality LLCs in diverse higher education contexts.

This book's new BPM highlights the importance of academic and residential relationships, reorienting the BPM in ways that offer clear guidance for practice. Rather than foregrounding the structure and programming of an LLC, the new version of the model centers student experiences within the LLC. This should lead to even more generative planning and assessment conversations based on the model – shifting attention from who is responsible for activities ("Is this curricular or co-curricular?") to how to create environments that create rich opportunities for student intellectual and social connection ("When and why will students engage with peers and faculty about this LLC theme?").

This edition also introduces new typologies of practice for every component of the BPM model. These typologies outline foundational, intermediate, and advanced attributes for each typology, providing research-informed guidance for practitioners at any stage of LLC development. For example, the infrastructure typology describes how key resources related to infrastructure (physical space, personnel, and funding) can be designed for maximum outcomes. Foundationally, the physical space in the LLC should have students living in the same residence hall to ensure living and learning in close proximity. In the advanced infrastructure stage, students are assigned to the same wing/floor/cluster and these rooms are clearly identified as part of the LLC. This helps students connect to the LLC and have a sense of identity as a community. A similar progression is seen in the social typology, where students start by attending LLC events and then move to planning and leading those events for (and beyond) the LLC and beyond in the advanced stage.

These BPM model typologies offer concrete guidance for LLC design, implementation, communication, and assessment. For example, if an institution is just starting out with LLCs, the typologies clearly describe the various components necessary to build a strong foundation for an effective LLC program. Once the institution has a more established structure, it can enhance its students' experiences by pursuing some of the more advanced features described in the typologies. For instance, the social typology can help an institution clarify its communication with students about why they might want to supplement their ongoing community service (or other thematic) activities by choosing to live in a relevant LLC.

The new BPM also rethinks the position and role of assessment in LLCs. Previously seen as the "mortar between the bricks," assessment is now connected to outcomes and has its place at the pinnacle of the new BPM. Assessing outcomes is crucial for ongoing improvement of LLCs and in determining the efficacy of programs and guiding resource allocation. And like the other typologies in this book, assessment is described at three levels to guide and inspire action for new and mature LLCs. The new "LLC Logic Model" (Figure 7.3) is a particularly significant contribution of this book, providing a solid scholarly scaffolding for short-, medium-, and long-term assessment of LLCs. With its new position in the BPM, assessment serves as a guide to help administrators – and everyone involved in residential education – develop assessment plans for LLC programs overall and for individual elements.

Finally, this book provides diverse, inspiring examples of practice to illustrate the BPM in action. As these examples reveal, the BPM provides a roadmap for intentionality about the physical location and design of LLCs, how students are assigned and supported in LLCs, and how faculty and staff lead them. This is not easy work, yet the institutional examples throughout this book give concrete guidance – and hope – for the transformative potential of LLCs.

The revised BPM for LLCs is not only immensely helpful for anyone interested in high-quality undergraduate education, but also is a foundation for making the case for the unique value of residential education. LLCs designed with the BPM blueprint will create an integrated intellectual and social student experience that enables all students to learn, connect, and thrive.

MarQuita Barker,
Vice President for Student Development,
Knox College, USA.

Peter Felten,
Assistant Provost for Teaching and Learning,
Executive Director, Center for Engaged Learning,
Elon University, USA.

REFERENCE

Mayhew, M. J., Rockenbach, A. N., Bowman, N. A., & Wolniak, G. C. (2016). *How college affects students: 21st century evidence that higher education works* (Vol. 3). San Francisco, CA: Jossey-Bass.

Acknowledgments

We are grateful to all of those who participated in and provided support for this project. To Jessie Moore and the Elon University Center for Engaged Learning, thank you for the initial opportunity that brought us together and for giving us space at CEL research seminar conferences to further share and explore living-learning communities. We also extend our appreciation to the 2017–2019 Center for Engaged Learning Research Seminar on Residential Learning Communities as a High-Impact Practice participants and co-leaders whose work was instrumental in informing this book. Additionally, we thank all of the living-learning community faculty and staff who graciously gave of their time to provide us with information about their individual programs that serve as examples throughout this book. We are fortunate to have such great colleagues who are committed to this work.

Chapter 1

Introduction to Living-Learning Communities in Practice

The landscape of postsecondary education in the United States is changing at a rapid pace. The rise of online education, changes in student demographics – with students trending older and more racially and ethnically diverse, and patterns of college-going (Snyder et al., 2018) have led some to wonder if brick and mortar colleges will continue to dot the landscape of the United States (Belkin, 2020). Others are more confident in the future of postsecondary education. In a speech at the EDUCAUSE conference in 2018, Ted Mitchell, president of the American Council on Education, quipped that it is once again fashionable to predict the demise of colleges and universities; he indicated that doing so is a pattern that repeats itself about every 30 years. Mitchell went on to describe how postsecondary education will adapt to change as opposed to being quashed by it. Among the solutions he advanced were to enhance engagement among students and faculty in order to increase student success.

The COVID-19 pandemic highlighted the importance of student engagement. Early research on the impact of the pandemic indicated that college students experienced exacerbated mental health struggles at the advent of COVID, with students reporting increases in depression, stress, and anxiety (Wang et al., 2020). Many students pointed to academic concerns as a primary stressor, and focused on the shift to online classes as a primary source of stress. These students sought coping mechanisms including support from the community, family, and friends as the primary way they were addressing the stress, anxiety, and depression they felt. In other words, enhanced engagement with others ameliorated their despair. When thoughtfully conceived and expertly delivered, living-learning communities (LLCs) can promote the exact type of faculty and peer engagement associated with student success. Doing so will help to quell lingering concerns about the benefit of brick and mortar institutions to society.

Learning communities are identified as an "official" High Impact Practice (Kuh, 2008) – research-supported initiatives that lead to student success in higher education. The natural elements of learning communities that classify them as high impact include investment of student time and effort, interaction with peers and faculty around important issues, experience with diversity, helpful and frequent feedback, integrative learning opportunities, and real-world applications of learning (Zilvinskis et al., 2022). LLCs are one specific type of learning community that provides experiences that meet these criteria and also a specifically structured environment for the experiences to happen within and beyond the classroom. Before proceeding further, we would like to note that we will be using the descriptor "living-learning communities" (or LLCs) throughout this book. Others may refer to these programs with other labels, such as residential learning communities, living-learning programs, and residential academic programs, but to be consistent, we will be referring to these units as LLCs.

By integrating living and learning, time and effort on purposeful tasks is likely to be increased, depending on how the LLCs are coordinated. Those that expect student participation in courses or activities such as service learning require the kind of involvement that may result in valuable outcomes. LLCs also provide opportunities for students to interact with faculty and other students for extended periods of time while addressing important topics. That time may be for a semester, a year, or longer in the case of Residential Colleges. As well, because they live together, peer interactions are substantial. While a commonality is what typically draws students to a LLC, such as a common major or interest, there is still the opportunity for diversity experiences and interactions with others who are different from them. Regardless of the focus of the LLC, diversity and inclusion can be intentional goals achieved through the structure of the LLC. Particularly if there is a course involved, but also through assessed activities, students can receive the requisite frequent feedback that is a hallmark of HIPs through their LLC. These are just a few of the elements of HIPs that program leaders can capitalize on to elevate the LLC experience.

THE ORIGINAL 2018 BEST PRACTICES MODEL

Not all learning communities, and not all LLCs, are high-impact. Intentional structuring of the program to include the high-impact factors is necessary for the types of outcomes sought through LLCs. In 2018, we published the original LLC Best Practices Model (BPM) in *Living-Learning Communities that Work: A Research-based Model for Design, Delivery, and Assessment* (Inkelas et al., 2018). The BPM is based on Maslow's (1954/1987) work, which posits that human motivation is based on a hierarchy of needs that he depicts as a pyramid. At the base of Maslow's pyramid are physiological needs (air, food, water, shelter, etc.), which he describes as the most basic for human functioning. The next level up on the pyramid includes human needs of safety (such as feelings of security, safety, and health), which, Maslow argues, can only be attended to once the basic needs are fulfilled. Each successive level of the human needs pyramid is built from the previous level, implying that higher order needs on the pyramid depend on lower levels for support.

The 2018 LLCs BPM is depicted in Figure 1.1. Readers will find a full description of the original BPM in *Living-Learning Communities That Work*; what follows is a condensed version that is intended to provide context for revisions to the model and for the work done thus far that utilized the original model (and prompted the revision). The base of the BPM pyramid is the **Infrastructure** of an LLC. The Infrastructure consists of four building blocks: the first block – and the cornerstone of the pyramid – is clear goals and objectives. Effective LLCs must have clear goals and objectives that not only align with the theme of the community but also permeate every other aspect of the model. In other words, the goals and objectives of an LLC should be the first thing considered when addressing every other aspect of the model, whether it be the collaboration among principal stakeholders, academic programming, or cocurricular activities. The two blocks that form the center of the infrastructure level of the pyramid represent a collaboration between the Academic Affairs unit responsible for the LLC and the Residence Life/Housing (RLH) Office at the institution. Because LLCs are academic programs that operate within residence halls, it is critical that these two functional areas, Academic Affairs and RLH, work together to develop and maintain the community. Finally, the last block in the infrastructure level is adequate resources, which includes human, physical, and financial resources.

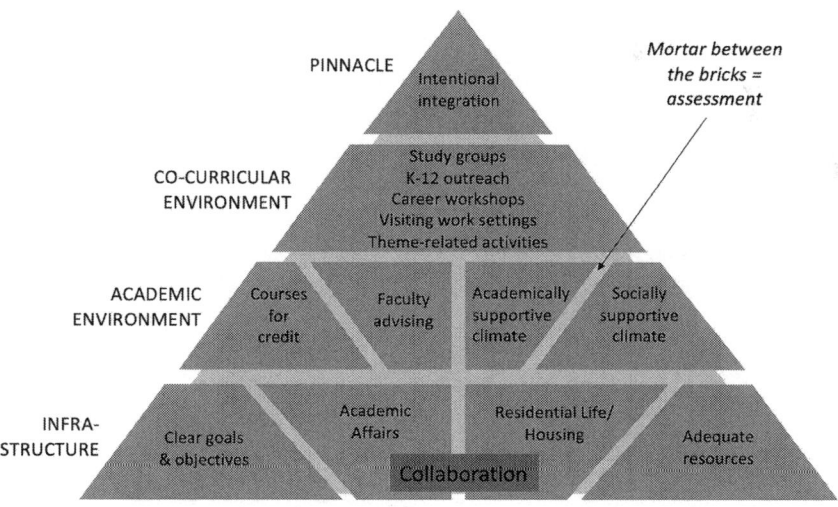

Figure 1.1 The Original Living-Learning Communities Best Practices Model (Inkelas et al., 2018).

On top of the infrastructure in the BPM is the next level of the pyramid: the **Academic Environment**. Similar to the Maslow model, the effectiveness of the academic environment depends on the infrastructure below it as a solid foundation. The academic environment consists of (a) courses for credit, (b) faculty advising, and (c) an academically and socially supportive climate. Academic courses provide an LLC an intellectual grounding, and offering them for credit ensures that students will take them seriously. Faculty involvement in an LLC, we argued, was beneficial, especially if it focused on the most common ways they participated in LLCs: teaching courses and advising students. Because most LLCs cater to first-year students, participants tended to see faculty in more traditional roles, but upon interacting with them more often in the LLC, those traditional boundaries could expand to deeper mentoring relationships. Finally, the last two blocks in the academic environment level pertained to how students perceived the climate in their residence halls. Of all of the aspects of an LLC, peer-to-peer relationships were the most powerful influence. And, given the nature of living and learning together, positive residence hall climates include those that support students academically and are socially supportive and fun.

The third level of the BPM is the **Cocurricular Environment**, or the out-of-class activities that reinforce the LLC's goals and objectives. Naturally, the success of the cocurricular environment depends on the academic environment and residence hall climate upon which it rests, and in general, the strongest cocurricular activities are those that align with and enhance the community's theme. For example, an Environmental Sustainability LLC might take its students on a field trip to a recycling plant or sponsor a community service event to clean up a local riverbed. In addition, findings from the National Study of Living-Learning Programs (Inkelas & Associates, 2004, 2008) showed that four cocurricular activities in particular were consistently linked to stronger student outcomes, including (a) study groups, (b) outreach to K-12 schools, (c) career workshops, and (d) visits to work settings.

The final level of the BPM, or the **Pinnacle**, consists of intentional integration, or the extent to which all of the other blocks in the model were aligned with the LLC's goals and objectives and with one another. Thus, the courses offered by the LLC should not only align with the community's goals and objectives but also dovetail with the cocurricular activities and the ways in which the LLC's faculty are involved. Similarly, the academic and social climate of the residence hall in which the LLC students live is not only influenced by the students themselves but also the staff and faculty who work directly with the community. Last but not least, **Assessment** comprised the "mortar between the bricks" that holds the LLC together. In order for effective LLCs to remain effective, they must continually evaluate their work, and the BPM provides the framework for what should be assessed.

REACTIONS TO THE FIRST BOOK

The original LLC BPM (Inkelas et al., 2018) has traveled through speaking engagements across the country and the world. The authors have keynoted several national conferences, including those that focus on a variety of LLCs, such as the Residential College Symposium, the Residential Learning Communities as a High-Impact Practice Conference, the ACUHO-I Academic Initiatives Conference, and the Learning Communities Association Summit. The model served as a keystone of the Elon University Center for Engaged Learning Research Seminar on Residential Learning Communities. We have also given plenary sessions at the annual meetings of several national academic and student affairs professional associations, including the Higher Learning Commission Conference, the HBCU Summit/Association of Public & Land Grant Universities, the Association of College & University Housing Officers – International, and the ACPA Residential Curriculum Institute. We have served as guests on higher education podcasts, facilitators and panelists on webinars, and have been asked to consult with universities on their LLCs using the BPM at campuses as diverse as the University of Colorado – Boulder, Rider University, and Indiana University of Pennsylvania. Our work has also been recognized by leading architectural firms specializing in college housing, and they have used elements of the BPM to advise architects on how to infuse living and learning elements into their residence hall and campus master plan proposals. Finally, the original BPM has even been overseas, particularly in Asia, where Karen Inkelas has keynoted conferences at the National University of Singapore, Sungkyunkwan University in Seoul, South Korea, and the University of Macau.

Throughout these speaking engagements, we have received positive feedback from audience members and other key stakeholders who have told us how they have used the BPM at their institutions to augment their LLC work. Particular attention has been focused on the following aspects:

Infrastructure

One popular form of feedback from audience members is that the infrastructure level of the BPM was instrumental in setting up a strong foundation for their LLCs. For some, this meant helping campus leadership to understand the justification for why academic affairs units and housing and residence life units must collaborate to create and maintain effective LLCs. Indeed, others mentioned that the three-part infrastructure framework of (1) goals and objectives; (2) a collaboration between RLH and other student affairs professionals; and (3) adequate resources was helpful in framing necessary elements of LLCs to senior leadership (e.g., deans, faculty, senior level administrators) in terms of funding and organizational structure. Still others took the recommendation that LLC goals and objectives be measurable, and re-aligned their LLCs with the AAC&U VALUE rubrics (AAC&U, n.d.) so that they would be able to use the rubrics to assess their communities.

Academic Environment

For some, the very existence of an academic environment was a new way to envision their LLCs. While most with whom we spoke recognized the value of involving faculty in their LLCs, they were unsure of what specific roles faculty would play in a living-learning community. The BPM argued persuasively to allow faculty to provide academic advice and support, instead of initially having faculty serve in more social capacities that they may feel uncomfortable with, such as dining with students, accompanying students on outings, or simply "hanging out" with students.

Perhaps the portion of the BPM that received the most interest was the advocacy for offering courses for credit as part of an LLC academic environment. Campus leaders or audience members often asked about this aspect of the model, including whether it was absolutely necessary for an LLC to offer courses for credit, or if providing academic content in other ways (guest speakers, discussion forums, etc.) would be an acceptable substitute. Still others inquired as to which specific types of courses would be best to include as part of the community – with options ranging from courses offered in the institution's general curriculum (e.g., Introductory courses), special small seminars developed specifically for the community, to "University 101" or "Introduction to our LLC" classes. These conversations generated some of the best discussions as we unveiled the model to various audiences.

Cocurricular Environment

Many with whom we interacted shared that the cocurricular environment was the portion of the original BPM with which they most resonated. Nearly all acknowledged the key role that cocurricular programming played in their LLCs, and were eager to share with others in the audience some of the more effective programming they had developed over the years. Many named programs that took advantage of the location of their campus – whether it be going to museums in the adjacent city or arranging hikes or nature outings in nearby natural areas or state parks. Still others talked about how they capitalized on the talents and interests of their faculty, who served as docents for the tours of the museums or nature guides on the hikes.

Others used the BPM to develop new cocurricular programming that was found to be effective in other communities: several noted the creation of a variety of K-12 school partnerships such as after school tutoring opportunities, Big Brother/Sister-Little Brother/Sister programs, and "Campus Days," in which

LLCs would invite the K-12 students and their families to spend a day at their university (often run in tandem with a broader university event). Still others, based on empirical linkages between study groups, career workshops, and visits to work settings and positive student outcomes, created more robust peer-advising programs and internship opportunities in partnership with community contacts.

Pinnacle

In what was often described as one of the most difficult portions of the BPM to achieve, some readers and audience members stated that they were working toward a more intentionally integrated LLC and that its appearance in the model gave them justification when explaining to their collaborators and stakeholders why communication across the LLC was so crucial. Indeed, the pinnacle of intentional integration was often mentioned as a beacon for why the various constituencies inside the LLC must share programming, whether it be why the faculty teaching the LLC courses should partner with the LLC's activities or why it was critical that the staff developing the cocurricular programs be aware of the interests and wishes of their student residents.

Assessment

Even assessment, the "mortar between the bricks" of the BPM, sometimes received accolades as a constant reminder that LLCs must continually evaluate its community. Finally, in what might be the most gratifying thing we learned about the BPM, one LLC professional told us how they used the model to identify which aspects of its LLC it needed to assess and ultimately developed a four-year assessment plan, with one-year focused on each level of the model.

ORGANIZATION OF THIS BOOK

In addition to positive feedback, we heard from audiences and stakeholders about the ways in which the 2018 BPM did not match up with their experiences as LLC practitioners. In Chapter 2, we highlight that feedback, as well as introduce the revised BPM and the rationale for the changes in the model.

In Chapters 3 through 8, we will not only further describe the revised levels of the BPM pyramid but also provide three additional features to help practitioners along their LLC journeys. The first feature, which is embedded in each chapter, consists of examples from actual LLCs that are illustrative of the various aspects of the model. However, it is important to understand that many of the examples we provided were obtained from LLC professionals prior to and during the COVID-19 pandemic. Given the systemic disruption that the pandemic caused throughout U.S. higher education, some of the examples (and staffing) may have changed significantly. The second feature, also embedded in each chapter, is a continuum, or a typology, of practices that can show LLCs how to move from providing a basic level of implementation for each level of the pyramid to more advanced levels of practice that optimally reinforce and enhance each portion of the model. The third feature, found in Chapter 7, which discusses assessment and outcomes, is the introduction of a logic model to frame both formative and summative aspects of LLCs. Logic models illustrate ways of moving from the status quo to aspirations.

In Chapter 9, we offer concluding thoughts to help institutions progress toward their aspirational goals. We also note lessons learned from the COVID-19 pandemic, and how those lessons offer ideas worth keeping for LLCs. We end with a discussion of the future of LLCs in American higher education's 21st century.

We are grateful to all of those who offered their thoughts and feedback about the original BPM, feedback that informed and resulted in the revised BPM unveiled in this volume. In the next chapter, that feedback and the revised model will be shared, providing a context for the description of each level of the revised model in the chapters to follow.

REFERENCES

Association of American Colleges & Universities. (n.d.). *VALUE Rubrics*. Retrieved from https://www.aacu.org/value-rubrics

Belkin, D. (2020, November 12). Is this the end of college as we know it? *The Wall Street Journal*. Retrieved from https://www.wsj.com/articles/is-this-the-end-of-college-as-we-know-it-11605196909

Inkelas, K. K., & Associates. (2004). *National Study of Living-Learning Programs: 2004 report of findings*. Retrieved July 17, 2006, from National Study of Living-Learning Programs website: http://www.livelearnstudy.net/images/NSLLP_2004_Final_Report.pdf

Inkelas, K. K., & Associates. (2008). *National Study of Living-Learning Programs: 2007 report of findings*. Retrieved August 28, 2008, from National Study of Living-Learning Programs website: http://www.livelearnstudy.net/images/2007_NSLLP_Final_Report.pdf

Inkelas, K. K., Jessup-Anger, J., Benjamin, M., & Wawrzynski, M. (2018). *Living-learning communities that work: A research-based model for design, delivery, and assessment*. Sterling, VA: Stylus Publishing, LLC.

Kuh, G. D. (2008). *High-impact educational practices: What they are, who has access to them, and why they matter*. Washington, DC: Association of American Colleges and Universities.

Maslow, A. (1954/1987). *Motivation and personality*. New York: Harper/Addison-Wesley.

Snyder, T. D., de Brey, C., & Dillow, S. A. (2018). *Digest of Education Statistics 2016* (NCES 2017-094). National Center for Education Statistics, Institute of Education Sciences, U.S. Department of Education. Washington, DC.

Wang, X., Hegde, S., Son, C., Keller, B., Smith, A., & Sasangohar, F. (2020). Investigating mental health of US college students during the Covid-19 pandemic: Cross-sectional survey study. *Journal of Medical Internet Research, 22*(9), E22817. doi: 10.2196/22817

Zilvinskis, J., Kinzie, J., Daday, J., O'Donnell, K., & Vande Zande, C. (2022). *Delivering on the promise of high-impact practices: Research and models for achieving equity, fidelity, and scale.* Sterling, VA: Stylus.

Chapter 2

The Revised Living-Learning Communities Best Practices Model

Although, as described in Chapter 1, initial reaction to the Best Practices Model (BPM) was positive, continued interaction with living-learning community (LLC) stakeholders using the BPM in practice helped our thinking about the model to evolve – as did the model itself. Those same campus leaders and audience members who spoke with us at the various conferences, consultancies, and other engagements with their affirmative feedback also questioned us constructively about portions of the model that did not align with their own experiences. In addition, one of the authors (Karen Inkelas) became the principal of a residential college after the original BPM was published; her experiences living in and directing her college and moving from theory to practice forced her to re-think aspects of the model. Through these conversations and experiences, it became clear that the following components of the BPM needed to be re-addressed:

- The partnership between Academic Affairs and Residence Life & Housing in the Infrastructure level of the pyramid required collaboration between the two units in order for the LLC to remain robust, but each unit also needed to focus on maintaining its own sustainability. Moreover, sustainability required attention to be paid during every portion of the life of an LLC, from the recruitment of new students, to the engagement of current students, to a positive regard held for the LLC from alumni, key stakeholders, and institutional leaders.
- Titling the two middle levels of the pyramid, the "Academic" and "Cocurricular" environments, tended to artificially foreground what an LLC *does* instead of what an LLC *is*. In other words, it emphasized – perhaps too heavily – the LLC's programming and not its people and its milieu.
- Moreover, two of the blocks within the Academic Environment may have been too prescriptive. The first block concerns academic courses for credit. Some have asked why the courses needed to be for credit. Others inquired

if it is necessary for all LLC members to take the courses. Still others have questioned if courses are the only way to insert academic content into an LLC. The second block addressed is the role of faculty as merely advisors, and some have argued that faculty roles in LLCs could be reimagined to be more inclusive, including various functions ranging from leadership positions to champions at the university level.

- Focusing narrowly on Academic and Cocurricular environments also tends to under-acknowledge the key roles that students and the social experience play in the life of an LLC. For many students, the most impactful element of an LLC is their peers – whether it be peer leaders like resident assistants or hall council presidents or simply neighbors on the floor. Indeed, for many students, the social experience is what gives them a sense of belonging or fellowship to the community, through its traditions, social events, and even simple peer interactions.
- Finally, in the original model, aspects of the residence hall climate were sandwiched into the academic environment, where some argued it did not fit, nor did it properly emphasize the crucial significance of the climate in the LLC. Some believed that the climate needed to be its own level of the pyramid, since it had a noteworthy impact on the health of an LLC.

Two of the authors (Jody Jessup-Anger and Mimi Benjamin) worked with a three-year, multi-institution research seminar on residential learning communities (RLCs) as a high-impact practice as part of Elon University's Center for Engaged Learning. Because the members of the research seminar worked closely with the BPM during their three-year study of RLCs, they were in an excellent position to offer us advice on how the model worked (or did not work) on their campuses and what changes to the model they would recommend. The research seminar participants provided us invaluable insight with thoughtful and thought-provoking perspectives, which became instrumental in reshaping the model.

- In terms of the Infrastructure, the seminar participants noted that adequate resources, such as human, physical, and financial resources, play a central role as the "basic needs" of LLCs. Indeed, without these crucial properties, there really is no LLC! Yet, in the original BPM, it occupies a small space in the corner of the base layer.
- Moreover, the placement of Academic Affairs and Residence Life & Housing as discrete blocks in the Infrastructure level may lead some to falsely believe that the influence of these two units does not stretch beyond the base layer of the pyramid. In fact, in an effective LLC, Academic Affairs and Residence Life & Housing have a major impact on all other aspects of the model in all of the other layers.

- On the other hand, the seminar participants did not want us to lose the original portion of the model that emphasized a collaboration between Academic Affairs and Residence Life & Housing. While the two units may initially have different goals and objectives for the LLC and they may independently influence the other layers of the pyramid, in order to be effective, they must collaborate at some level on the infrastructure plane.
- Similar to the feedback we received from our presentations, the seminar participants felt that the model did not adequately represent the role of peers in an LLC. Many felt that peers "make or break" the LLC experience and thus should be incorporated more explicitly into the BPM.
- Further, like the viewpoints of audience members and campus leaders, they also felt that faculty roles in the LLC can and should be expanded to represent more than merely advising.
- Finally, the seminar participants questioned whether assessment really is the "mortar between the bricks" that holds the whole model together. While they acknowledged the importance of assessment in maintaining a healthy and effective LLC, some argued that communication is actually the glue that holds the LLC together. This type of communication includes all of the LLC's major stakeholders: staff, faculty, students, and external community members.

THE REVISED 2018 BEST PRACTICES MODEL

With such a rich tapestry of recommendations to work from, we experimented with several different revisions to the BPM until we designed one that we felt encapsulated all of the insightful feedback we received. We are delighted to unveil the revised Living-Learning Communities Best Practices Model in Figure 2.1.

The first notable change is that there are no longer discrete blocks in the revised model. Instead, the new model represents a unified pyramid to symbolize how all of the levels of the model interact with one another seamlessly. Despite the lack of blocks, however, the implied hierarchy – similar to Maslow's hierarchy – is still in effect. Higher levels of the revised model still depend upon the support they receive from the levels below them in the pyramid.

Infrastructure

Another major change to the model is that Academic Affairs and Residence Life & Housing are no longer discrete blocks, but instead are infused throughout the entire model. Represented by the gradient shading in the lower left corner of the Infrastructure level, the influence of Academic Affairs units permeates the entire model, but exists most strongly in the Infrastructure level where it shares direct responsibility for providing the LLC resources as well as offers the LLC its

THE REVISED LIVING-LEARNING COMMUNITIES BEST PRACTICES MODEL

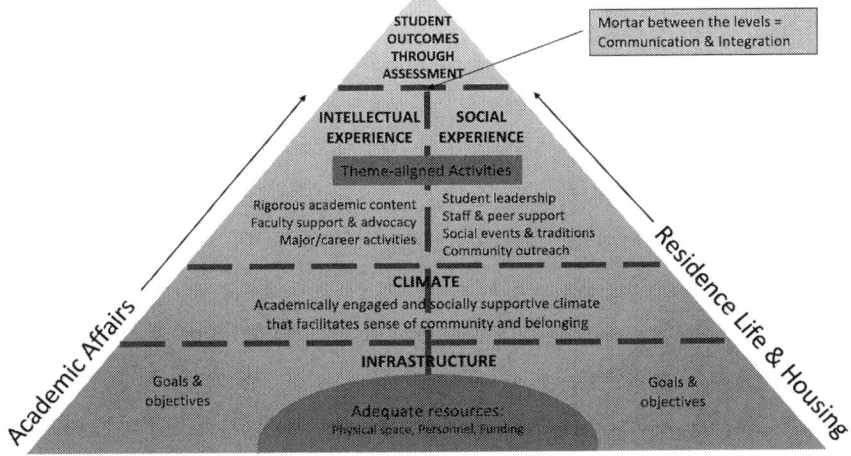

Figure 2.1 The Revised Living-Learning Communities Best Practices Model.

own distinctive goals and objectives. Similarly, Residence Life & Housing influences the entire model, and most strongly exists in the lower right corner of the Infrastructure level – where it shares responsibility for providing the LLC's resources and offers its own distinctive goals and objectives. The two units do, however, come together to collaborate, as shown by the area where they intersect, just above the semi-circle depicting the LLC's resources.

The Infrastructure level in the revised model now places Adequate Resources prominently in the center, visually providing the central importance of resources to the LLC – as was asserted by members of the Elon research seminar. The Adequate Resources portion of the model is immediately adjacent to both the Academic Affairs and Residence Life & Housing virtual cornerstones of the Infrastructure layer of the pyramid, representing the optimal contribution of both units in providing the resources for the LLC. As with the original model, necessary resources include physical space, personnel, and funding. An expanded description of important resources for LLCs can be found in Chapter 3.

Climate

Audience members, campus leaders, and the Elon seminar participants questioned whether the residence hall climate was appropriately placed in the Academic Environment layer of the original BPM. Several felt that the climate neither belonged in a layer about academic aspects of the LLC nor was given enough prominence in the model. Indeed, some felt that the residence hall climate was so important to the health of an LLC that it was more of a "basic" need: without a robust academic and social climate in the LLC, there would not be strong student engagement with the community's programs and activities, and the students would not find the community to be supportive.

Consequently, in the revised model, the Climate of the LLC has become its own layer of the pyramid, directly above the Infrastructure. Similar to the Maslow hierarchy, the Climate is placed on top of the Infrastructure level because an LLC cannot develop a distinctive climate without its "basic needs" of Adequate Resources and an Academic Affairs and Residence Life & Housing partnership. On the other hand, an academically and socially supportive climate can be thought of as serving as a prerequisite to all academic and social programming that is created within the LLC: if students (and staff) do not feel as though there is a supportive climate in the LLC that encourages engagement with one another, no amount of programming will be successful because it will not garner active and enthusiastic participation. Thus, LLCs should strive to facilitate an academically engaging and socially supportive climate that facilitates in its participants a strong sense of belonging to the community. Additional description of the climate, including how to create and sustain it, is found in Chapter 4.

Intellectual and Social Experience

The next level of the BPM pyramid is split in two: intellectual experiences and social experiences. They are not stacked one on top of another because we find them to be equally essential and mutually reinforcing. Both the intellectual and social experiences should be, as much as possible, theme-aligned so that the goals and objectives of the LLC remain threaded through all of the experiences. And, as described earlier, it is important to note that, while Intellectual Experience is placed on the side of the pyramid closer to Academic Affairs than Residence Life & Housing, both units contribute to the intellectual life of the LLC. Yet, it is generally assumed that Academic Affairs will have more of an influence on the intellectual experience than the social. Similarly, both Residence Life & Housing and Academic Affairs contribute to the social life of their LLC, but it is expected that Residence Life & Housing plays a larger role in this domain.

Among the Intellectual Experiences, the portion of the original BPM that required LLCs to offer courses for credit as a best practice is now replaced with "Rigorous academic content." Numerous LLC practitioners, as well as our own experience, taught us that intellectual content can come in many forms, and it does not necessarily involve courses for credit. That being said, for-credit courses are still optimal for LLCs and remain a definitive way to infuse rigorous academic content into a residential learning community. However, other activities, such as guest lectures, discussion series, and service learning opportunities, can also augment the intellectual experience in an LLC. Chapter 5 will describe a continuum of academic possibilities that LLCs can introduce to enhance their intellectual atmosphere.

THE REVISED LIVING-LEARNING COMMUNITIES BEST PRACTICES MODEL

The role of faculty in the LLC has also expanded to include more than mere advising. Instead, we acknowledge the many ways in which faculty engage with their LLCs, including serving not only as advisors but also as teachers, administrators, champions, mentors, learners, and more. Finally, several of the former Cocurricular Activities from the original model are included in the Intellectual Experience portion of the revised model: study groups, career workshops, and visits to work settings are retained, with the latter two being subsumed under "Major/career activities."

The Social Experience portion of the BPM is the only part of the revised model that is entirely new. Several practitioners and members of the Elon research seminar underscored the critical importance of the social environment in an LLC and lamented its absence in the BPM. Many also argued that the social environment was as important as, if not more important than, the academic environment. Accordingly, in this revised version of the BPM, the Social Experience is placed side-by-side with its counterpart, the Intellectual Experience. In the Social Experience, the influence of peers – another aspect of LLCs that many told us was missing in the original model – is now given a prominent place in the model through peer support and fellowship. Peer support can be either formal or informal: peers may fulfill official roles, such as resident assistants (RAs) or peer mentors, or they may simply be friendships formed in the residence hall. Social events and traditions, such as banquets, holiday celebrations, and friendly competitions, occupy an extremely important place in the life of an LLC. They help to bring a continuity and history to the LLC when repeated, and can serve as the tangible manifestation of a healthy and socially supportive climate. Finally, community outreach (which includes K-12 outreach from the original model) expands upon the idea of working with the surrounding community in ways that dovetail with the goals and objectives of the LLC, and is placed in this portion of the model in recognition that it is the students who are making the connections with the broader community. Additional description of the new Social Experience aspect of the revised model is found in Chapter 6.

Student Outcomes through Assessment

In the original BPM, Assessment was thought of as the "mortar between the bricks," or the component of the model that held the rest of the blocks together. In the revised model, Student Outcomes through Assessment takes its place as the pinnacle, or the portion of the model that rests on top of all of the other layers. Outcomes assessment's placement atop the pyramid in the revised model is symbolic of its role of being comprehensive in its perspective; LLCs should strive to assess all of the other facets of the BPM, and should use the information gained from their data to improve and innovate their offerings. Chapter 7 provides information about this element of the BPM.

Integration and Communication

Although Assessment is no longer seen as the "mortar" and the pyramid is now depicted as unified and not composed of discrete blocks, this does not mean that the concept of the mortar that holds the BPM together has disappeared. Instead, we followed the advice of the Elon research seminar participants and revised the mortar to consist of Integration and Communication. The participants agreed that integration of the various parts of the original model was essential for an effective LLC. However, they believed that integration was not an additive feature that sat atop the pyramid, but should be depicted instead as a concept that was interwoven through all of the blocks in the model. Similarly, they argued that the way to ensure that all of the parts of the model were integrated was to have effective communication among all of the stakeholders in the LLC: faculty, staff, and students. Consequently, the revised BPM also includes a "mortar" (Integration and Communication), but it is important to note that the new pyramid is permeable. One can move from one level or concept to another seamlessly in the new model. Thus, the "mortar" is seen as being more symbolic, as something woven into the pyramid instead of the substance that held the pyramid together. Accordingly, the mortar, discussed in Chapter 8, is now represented as dashed lines instead of a thick paste undergirding the entire model.

AN ASPIRATIONAL MODEL

One question that often arose when we introduced the original BPM to campus leaders and audiences big and small was whether an LLC that did not embody all of the aspects of the model was not, by default, a LLC. For example, if an LLC did not offer courses for credit, could it still consider itself an LLC? If its collaboration between Academic Affairs and Residence Life & Housing was really in name only, or if it did not conduct any assessment, was it even an LLC? Indeed, there was rigorous debate over whether all programs that called themselves "living-learning" were, indeed, LLCs.

It is our belief that LLCs that are missing some elements of the BPM are not disqualified from considering themselves to be, in fact, an LLC. What we believe is more important is that the LLC leadership acknowledge that there are areas of its structure that it needs to address in order to improve and become a better version of itself. In this sense, we conceive of the BPM as an aspirational model. The BPM provides a framework for LLC practitioners to work from when identifying the areas of their community that they need to develop, shore up, or change. No doubt, there is no such thing as the perfect LLC, and no LLC should denigrate the good work it is doing in pursuit of the perfect. That being said, the BPM offers an archetype – a model toward which all practitioners can aspire through different paths.

Chapter 3

Best Practices in Living-Learning Communities: Infrastructure

OVERVIEW OF THE INFRASTRUCTURE

As illustrated in Chapter 2 and depicted in Figure 3.1, the infrastructure layer of the revised living-learning community (LLC) Best Practices Model (BPM) provides the foundation of the pyramid. Without the foundational dimensions encompassed in this base layer, the LLC is likely not viable, and certainly not sustainable. The revised model places adequate resources at the center of the foundation because of their role as the "basic needs" of the LLC. On either side of the adequate resources dimension are the goals and objectives of Academic Affairs and Residence Life & Housing (RLH) respectively. These goals and objectives begin at the foundation of the pyramid but span through each layer to the pinnacle. Furthermore, although some of the goals and objectives of Academic

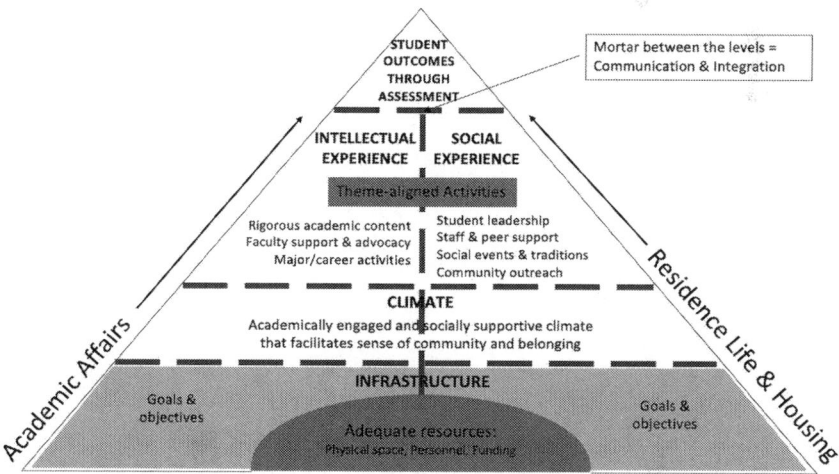

Figure 3.1 The Infrastructure of the Revised Best Practices Model.

Affairs and RLH may be distinct, they meet at the center of the infrastructure layer to indicate the importance of collaboration between them to the success of the community. Next we detail the specifics of each dimension of the infrastructure, provide a typology illustrating foundational, intermediate, and advanced levels of each dimension, and provide case study examples from our discussion with LLC administrators.

ADEQUATE RESOURCES

No college or university should initiate LLCs without first considering how to resource them. Although there is substantial variation in the resources needed to sustain these initiatives, there is research indicating that resources play a role in the quality of outcomes (Wawrzynski & Jessup-Anger, 2010) and anecdotal evidence that resources matter for sustainability.

Physical Space

At the risk of stating the obvious, the existence of the LLC rests on its physical presence. Physical spaces important for LLC delivery include residence hall rooms, faculty spaces, staff spaces, academic spaces, and common spaces, which might include dining facilities. Our interviews with LLC administrators demonstrated the vital role that LLC spaces play in successful administration of LLCs. Inadequate, ill-utilized, or poorly administered space can lead to unmet potential in LLCs.

Residence Hall Rooms

There are several considerations for LLC administrators when designating a hall, or portion of a hall, as an LLC and assigning students. First is the size of the hall relative to the size of the LLC. The reason this ratio matters is that it will determine whether the LLC conveys a dominant identity in the residence hall. In *Designing for Learning*, Carney Strange and James Banning (2015) detailed how the collective attributes of students can shape a learning environment. If the majority of students share an LLC identity, the LLC identity may be easily cultivated by the collective identity of the students. If, on the other hand, there are only a few LLC members in a hall comprised of otherwise unaffiliated students, LLC students will have a more difficult time differentiating who is in an LLC and who is not, which may make their LLC identity more distal. Also important are students' residence hall rooms, which arguably are where they will spend the most time while participating in the LLC.

As illustrated in the Infrastructure Typology (Figure 3.2), which lays out considerations for the infrastructure level of the BPM, the assignment of residence hall rooms serves as one physical dimension administrators should consider as they build or sustain LLCs. In the foundational category of the typology, students in the LLC are assigned to the same residence hall. This shared context will hopefully help them to bond with one another and begin to foster a collective LLC identity. A residential college coordinator at UNC-Greensboro (UNC-G) shared a sentiment common to many LLC administrators when he spoke of the competing priorities faced by housing professionals when they are trying to honor their commitment to LLCs. He explained that although students must be in the affiliated community in order to live in a particular hall (or room), exceptions are made for overflow housing, meaning that sometimes unaffiliated students find themselves in the community. The strategy employed by UNC-G when unaffiliated students are placed into LLCs is to recruit these students to join the community, which sometimes works. At UNC-G, there are no academic requirements to join the community, which makes integrating new members more seamless than if there were requirements. Another challenge arises when students want to live together, but only one wants to be in or is eligible for the LLC. Sometimes the requirements of the LLC may mean that a student needs to choose between participating or rooming with a friend or prior roommate. Administrators will need to decide how much fidelity in membership they maintain on a floor. In addition, LLC administrators will need to consider how saturated they want a student's experience to be. It is sometimes difficult for a student to live with peers, engage with them on the residence hall floor, and also have several classes with them (Jessup-Anger & Howell, 2021), especially if their values and those of their peers are at odds.

In the intermediate category of the typology, not only are LLC students paired together by hall, but they are also clustered together by wing or floor, which increases the likelihood that they develop a shared LLC identity that may help students bond and also serves to raise awareness about the LLC across campus, increasing the likelihood of sustainability. The director of residence life and assistant dean of students at St. Anselm College discussed the negotiation that takes place with Academic Affairs to ensure the space is right-sized for LLC use. She shared that the placement of the LLC typically happens in a building designated as the Living-Learning Commons, in which most LLCs are housed. However, sometimes the faculty directors have a compelling reason to ask for different space – perhaps they are targeting first-year students for a class, so a hall more heavily composed of first-year students makes more sense. Or, perhaps it is a small community, so a smaller cluster is a better fit. An example used from St. Anselm to illustrate the variation was Art House, which was assigned to a single apartment. In Art House, the students living there opened the bottom level of the apartment as a gallery space, which they used to showcase art when they occasionally opened the apartment up to an interested audience.

The flexibility in LLC assignments, from floors, to clusters, to rooms, can account for variation in size from year to year, increasing the likelihood of sustainability, and decreasing the chance that unaffiliated students will be placed in the community, which can create a sense of isolation for them and lessen a sense of community for affiliated students. Flexibility in assignments may also enable the LLC to become more established over time, which may lead to designation of a more permanent, dedicated space.

Permanent, dedicated space may ensure that students are clustered appropriately and common spaces are branded to communicate LLC themes, which is congruent with the advanced category of the LLC typology for residence hall space. In Inkelas et al. (2018), we detailed this configuration extensively in our case study of Pace University-Westchester. In Pace's new residence hall, Alumni Hall, each LLC (called First-Year Interest Groups, or FIGs) has its own wing, and each wing includes a centrally located lounge. Moreover, each lounge is decorated according to its theme: the Body and Mind FIG's lounge is outfitted as a yoga studio, while the Extreme Sports & Pace National (ESPN) FIG has a television viewing area that resembled a bowling niche, and includes ping-pong and foosball tables. Although having a dedicated and branded cluster, floor, or hall can help to convey LLC identity, it can be costly to change or alter if the LLC needs to move or proves unsustainable. Thus, it may be solely reserved for long-standing LLCs that are likely to persist over time.

LLC Faculty Space

As Jessup-Anger and Benjamin (2023) illustrated in their chapter in *The Faculty Factor: Developing Faculty Engagement with Living Learning Communities,* faculty may feel well outside their comfort zone in residence hall spaces. Especially if there are few public gathering spaces in a residence hall, inviting faculty into the hall without providing some physical space in which to engage might prove awkward for faculty and students alike. As depicted in the Infrastructure Typology (Figure 3.2) of the BPM, consideration of faculty spaces is another physical dimension that administrators should consider as they build or sustain LLCs. At the foundational level, faculty should have space in the residence hall they can reserve for meetings and know the process by which they can reserve the space. In Grogan Residential College at UNCG, for example, participants have priority over common space on the first floor of the building, but it is not designated exclusively for their use. The program chair of Grogan indicated that to ensure that space is available, he works with the hall director to maintain a calendar for space. Although he concedes that having an entire building dedicated to the residential college would be ideal, the resources provided and the systems in place to ensure access to those resources are helpful to the community.

At the intermediate level, faculty have designated office space in the residence hall where they can hold office hours, work, or meet with student groups. Having these designated spaces is helpful to faculty and students alike. For faculty, the designated space ensures they have a comfortable place in the hall in which to maintain a presence. For students, these spaces can guarantee they can bump into faculty, which might result in the informal interactions necessary to build more meaningful relationships (Cox & Orehovec, 2007; Sriram et al., 2020). In Inkelas et al. (2018), we detailed residential colleges that included spaces for faculty offices. In particular, faculty in James Madison College at Michigan State University indicated that having their offices in the building where students lived minimized barriers to student participation in office hours. Although universally appreciated by faculty with whom we spoke, several mentioned a potential downside – students would come to office hours or class in loungewear that they deemed a bit too casual for meeting with faculty. It seems that a conversation about boundaries and appropriate preparation for office hours and engagement with faculty at the outset of the year might be sufficient to ward off awkward encounters.

At the advanced level of the typology of LLC faculty space, faculty affiliated with the LLC live in the residence hall or on the premises in spaces designed for families. This model, with faculty – and faculty families in residence – ensures that faculty and student interaction occurs formally and informally. In addition, it provides a convenient way for faculty to seamlessly collaborate with other staff affiliated with the program. In Hereford Residential College at the University of Virginia, for example, the principal, who lives on the premises, is dedicated half-time to the RC, meaning that part of their time is spent teaching and researching in their home department and the rest is dedicated to administration of the residential college. The program coordinator, on the other hand, is full time with the RC. By having the principal of the RC on the premises, collaboration is more seamless. In addition, by having spaces that are adequate for families, with apartments that have two or three bedrooms, LLCs will have a deeper pool of candidates from which to draw. Often good candidates for LLC director positions are those who are more established scholars that have less to worry about in terms of promotion and tenure (Golde & Pribbenow, 2000). These scholars tend to be older and may have partners and families in tow.

LLC Staff Space

In our typology, we differentiate between faculty space and staff space. And, in addition, we conceptualize staff as those who provide administrative support to the community that is different from that provided by faculty and residence life staff. These staff may support admissions, programming, administrative functions, or a combination thereof. Like faculty spaces, we indicate in the typology that at the foundational level, LLC staff may reserve space in the residence hall for any function they perform. These functions may include meetings with students, programs, or other support functions. At the intermediate level, LLC staff have designated office space in the residence hall. This consistent physical presence can serve to promote collaboration with residence hall staff and faculty. It can also ensure that these staff are accessible to students and can serve as another seamless connection point for students to develop meaningful relationships. At the advanced level, LLC staff space is designated in the office and used regularly for meetings with faculty, staff, and students. This physical manifestation of collaboration encourages faculty and students to meet frequently, ensuring that they are in communication with one another.

Residence Hall Academic Space

Integrating living and learning is made infinitely easier if there are spaces in the residence hall for learning to occur. In a conversation with the associate dean of residential programs at Rider University, she illustrated how, at the foundational level, lounge space could be used to encourage students to engage with one another academically. She explained that there were several features of the lounges that encouraged students to collaborate, including a white board, tables, and chairs. She also shared that peer mentors were able to use the space for study sessions with students, which was convenient and likely made students more inclined to come to these sessions.

At the intermediate level, the classroom space exists in the hall and is designated for priority use by the LLC. The residential college coordinator at UNC-G indicated that their residential colleges have classroom space within their buildings and that LLCs are prioritized for use of the classroom space, especially when an entire building isn't dedicated to the LLC. When a classroom space is designated for LLC use and branded to the theme of the LLC, it is classified as advanced. We discussed the existence of these advanced residence hall academic spaces in Inkelas et al. (2018) with the example of science-focused Lyman Briggs College at Michigan State University. The Lyman Briggs website (https://lbc.msu.edu/about/index.html) highlights the smaller class sizes, dedicated faculty, and learning assistants who are all embedded in the community. In addition, the website boasts that Lyman Briggs students have the shortest commute possible, with coursework and labs embedded in the residence hall, necessitating that students only leave their rooms to attend classes and lab sections, which is likely especially appealing to students during cold Michigan winters.

Residence Hall Common Space

In addition to academic space in the residence hall, common space is a vital element of the infrastructure of an LLC. In order for students to bond with one another, they must be able to gather comfortably. The chair of the Department of Sport Management at Elon University described how the Sport Management and Media LLC made use of common spaces for their events. She indicated that although the LLC had no dedicated common space, they capitalized on their location beside a dining hall and patio area to hold events. This use of common space that is available to all illustrates the foundational level of common space use in the physical dimension of the infrastructure typology.

At the intermediate level is Hereford Residential College at the University of Virginia. The principal of the college explained that the common space is available for residents to use, and that if the need arises, the furniture could be rearranged to accommodate a seminar. However, she noted that the space is insufficient for college-wide events, as Hereford has upwards of 200 students enrolled.

At the advanced level for residence hall common space, the space is designated and branded for LLC use. Lyman Briggs College at Michigan State University provides a quintessential example of thoughtfully designed common space that is branded for LLC use. The CELL (Collaborative Experiential Learning Laboratory), which is located in the residence hall, "is equipped with a 3D printer and board games, Virtual Reality and glue sticks" (https://lbc.msu.edu/the-briggs-experience/cell.html). Among the items available for student use include a Cricut cutter, carving tools, and a jewelry making kit. According to the Lyman Briggs website, the space was initiated and designed by students from different disciplines with some guidelines to follow and resources to support them. The space has Open Hours for LLC students and is reservable by students and faculty alike.

As illustrated by the various facets of the typology, LLC administrators have a lot to consider regarding the physical space of the community. Especially if the LLC is in a shared building, there may be limitations on the amount of space designated specifically for the LLC. Making sure that shared common space is reservable, and that people connected with the LLC know how to reserve it, is a first step in providing the bonding spaces necessary for LLC engagement. In addition to space, it is important to consider personnel resources as a key feature of the infrastructure of the LLC.

Personnel

Although not all personnel need to have 100% of their time dedicated to LLC administration, the personnel associated with the community should all have a sense of what the community is and how their role interfaces with it. Personnel in student affairs that are connected to the LLC often include professional residence life staff situated in the building, resident assistants, and other student staff. In addition, there are often administrators with roles more distal, but no less important. These include residence life administrators and student affairs administrators. In addition to student affairs administrators, there should be personnel from Academic Affairs including faculty, and, ideally, Academic Affairs administrators as well.

Professional Residence Life Staff in the Building

Often, when we present at conferences about the need for the BPM, Jody shares a story about her early years as a hall director when she was placed in a building with an engineering LLC. The hall was advertised as an LLC but was composed of both LLC and non-LLC students. When she started as a hall director, no information was provided about the goals of the LLC, nor were there any structures in place to facilitate communication or collaboration between the hall staff and College of Engineering. The experience was akin to reading a mystery novel – trying to figure out the intended outcome with bread crumbs dropped along the way. We use this example to illustrate why best practices are needed for staffing and should be attended to as LLCs are developed and staff are onboarded when a staffing transition happens. At the foundational level of the typology, professional residence life staff in the building, such as a hall director or area coordinator, should understand and support the LLC goals and objectives. A faculty in residence at Elon shared how the policies and procedures developed in residence life ensure that this basic level of knowledge is passed along to professional residence life staff. She explained that there are overarching goals for the LLCs that are connected to university learning outcomes and some that are specific to the LLCs. From these goals, LLC directors craft a syllabus and submit it to residence life during the semester prior to implementation. These documents are shared with both the hall director and any RAs affiliated with the community. That process ensures that the foundational level of the typology is met.

In the intermediate level of the typology, the hall director works with hall staff to connect initiatives to the LLC theme. The director of residence life and assistant dean of students at St. Anselm College described how hall staff and LLC administrators work together. She explained that, at the outset of the academic year, she calls a meeting of RAs, the LLC program director, and any professional staff that are affiliated with LLC buildings. During the meeting the LLC director shares information about the curriculum, out-of-class meetings planned by the LLC, and other activities that will take place over the course of the semester. The hall staff identify ways they can support programming with their resources; these ways may include helping with logistics, booking a venue, or providing financial support. The meeting helps the LLC administrators more easily enact their vision, while also helping professional hall staff become knowledgeable about what the LLC is doing.

At the advanced level, the hall director and staff collaborate with the LLC faculty to achieve goals and objectives. Whereas at the intermediate level, one party or the other is driving the LLC theme, at the advanced level, professional staff and LLC administrators are working collaboratively to achieve these goals and objectives. An associate director of residence life we talked to shared how difficult it is to ensure that hall directors and other in-building staff in residence life are able to collaborate effectively with LLC faculty to achieve goals and objectives of the LLC. She indicated that in her time working with LLCs, the level of collaboration between the LLC and in-building professional staff had waxed and waned. The collaboration was highly dependent on staff in the in-building positions and also on residence life administration and their understanding of the LLC. She shared that the collaboration seemed to be more consistent when it was explicitly stated as part of staff responsibility.

Resident Assistant (RA) Student Staff

As with live-in professional staff, resident assistant staff move from foundational to more advanced levels of the typology, depending on the amount of integration and influence on the LLC. At the foundational level, resident assistants understand and support the LLC goals and objectives but aren't involved in connecting initiatives to the LLC theme.

At the intermediate level, the resident assistant works to connect initiatives to the LLC theme. The associate dean of residential programs at Rider University explained that in the science-themed LLC, they strive to have the RA (called Community Advisors at Rider) be a science major. And, when these student leaders implement required programming for the floor, they do so with the LLC theme in mind. She estimated that about half of the programs implemented in the community are theme-focused. She also emphasized that students in the LLC don't necessarily want the sole focus of their programming to be LLC-themed, and so the balance between themed events and general events is welcomed by students.

At the advanced level, resident assistants in the LLC collaborate with the LLC faculty to achieve goals and objectives of the community. At St. Anselm, RAs are utilized in achieving the goals and objectives of the LLC. The director of residence life at St. Anselm explained that, after meeting with key personnel in the beginning of the year, the LLC director stays in touch with the RAs and leans on them for support for cocurricular initiatives throughout the year. She indicated that it is common for RAs to get an email from the director encouraging them to spread the word about a speaker who will be on campus and a plea for them to help get LLC students there. When RAs get this information, they post flyers, invite students through the social media platform *Group Me,* and even knock on doors on their way to the program. It was clear from the director's description that the RAs are invested in ensuring LLC-administered programs are well attended.

Student Staff

In addition to resident assistants, LLCs often have other peer mentors or tutors affiliated with the community. In order to meet the standard of the Best Practice Model, these student staff should be compensated for their work at a rate that is commensurate with their duties. Without proper remuneration, students who must work for pay in order to attend college would be precluded from taking on this leadership position within the LLC. In addition, having volunteer mentors or tutors and paid RAs creates inequities that make working together difficult. At the foundational level, non-residence life student staff provide support for students as they would other students on campus. At this level, tutors from the writing center or math lab might spend a day of their office hours each week in the LLC.

At the intermediate level, peer staff are designated for the LLC and serve in live-out positions that support the goals and objectives of the LLC. These students might work in partnership with RAs, but their primary focus is on the academic aspect of the LLC. At Loyola Maryland, this type of role is held by Evergreen peer leaders, who are housed in the student engagement office at Loyola but serve as support to the LLCs. These students begin to work as peer mentors for incoming students at orientation and then stay with the LLC for the year, helping with weekly enrichment sessions that are connected to the LLCs. The associate director of Messina, an LLC aimed at promoting a smooth transition to college for first-year students, explained that the role of the Evergreen has shifted over time to work more effectively within the LLC structure. She indicated that, initially, Evergreens were charged with doing programming in the halls in addition to helping with enrichment sessions. The programming role ruffled feathers of some of the RAs who were uncomfortable that the Evergreen had a "fun" role to play in their space but took no responsibility for enforcing rules. As a result of feedback from RAs and Evergreens alike, the structure was changed so that Evergreens work primarily to support the academic and enrichment aspects of the LLC and the residential elements are left to the RAs.

At the advanced level, peer mentors, tutors, or other peer leaders are designated to support the LLC, live in the building, and support LLC objectives in both the residence hall and the classroom. At Rider, LLC-affiliated peer mentors were described as students who serve as peer tutors in the hall and support students academically in the LLC. Among their duties are holding tutoring hours in the lounge and keeping abreast of what is happening in the classroom. These students are supervised by the faculty director of the LLC as opposed to residence life staff. For remuneration, peer mentors get a more desirable room in the residence hall at a reduced rate. These peer mentors often lived together in these nicer rooms within the hall. This compensation, plus relationship building with the faculty director, was sufficient that there was no difficulty attracting students to these positions. The program chair of Grogan College at the University of North Carolina – Greensboro shared that Grogan also utilizes peer mentors in the community. These students, called community ambassadors, serve to mentor younger students in the program. He indicated that the community ambassadors are almost always second-year students in the program or juniors or seniors who have completed the two-year program. These students live in the community and their primary charge is to cultivate community, which they do in conjunction with RAs.

Residence Life Administration

In addition to live-in staff being invested in the LLC, it is important that the central administration in Residence Life & Housing is committed to supporting the community. At the foundational level, professional staff support LLC initiatives through housing assignments. One of our interviewees shared some frustration at the level of involvement of residence life in the LLCs with which she was affiliated. What she described met the criteria for foundational involvement from residence life administration. Aside from administering assignments, housing has little to do with programming at all, which she attributed to a sense of insularity on the part of the faculty who direct the program. This insularity made it difficult for residence life central staff to connect, which resulted in duplication of resources, particularly faculty time, as the residence life staff create their own academically focused programs and recruit different faculty to partake.

At the intermediate level, central residence life administrators are engaged in LLC administration oversight as one aspect of a broader job description. These residence life administrators can help to ensure continuity of the community over time by connecting hall directors to LLC academic personnel, providing guidance regarding housing assignments, and even championing budget and other resources to the community. The associate director of the residential student experience in University Housing at California Polytechnic University was one such position held by a person we interviewed. As housing was working to build and sustain LLCs, the associate director often established connections with academic advisors, career staff, and associate deans and faculty to ensure they understood the benefits of LLC work. To build capacity, she often positioned residence life and LLCs as potential supports to academic and faculty-driven initiatives, asking questions like, "What do you do in the first weeks of school that you want reinforced during midterms?" She offered LLCs as a place where the assistance they identified could be fostered. Once faculty and academic administrators saw the benefits of collaboration with residence life, they were much more inclined to partner.

One drawback of the intermediate level of residence life administration is that other demands, depending on what they are, can usurp the time that is dedicated to building relationships with Academic Affairs and LLC administrators because the role isn't dedicated solely to LLC development. Sometimes, when other priorities arise, or when unanticipated emergencies happen, the LLC relationship building and sustainability may seem less pressing. When this pattern develops, it may be difficult to regain traction in relationship building.

On the advanced level of central residence life administration, campus-wide LLC residential responsibilities are designated as a primary aspect of professional staff roles. Elon University has a position within residence life dedicated to building community partnerships. This position of Associate Director of Residence Life for Residential Education and Community Development works in conjunction with a university-level academic position titled Director of Academic-Residential Partnerships (described in more detail in the next section). The associate director of residence life for residential education and community development is a dual reporting position that reports both to the director of residence life and the director of academic-residential partnerships. It evolved from the decoupling of a position that also included training and development, which was deemed too large in scope to work effectively.

Student Affairs Administration

In addition to Residence Life & Housing personnel being instrumental to successful LLC administration, it is important that the student affairs administration across the division is also aware and supportive of LLC efforts. At the foundational level, student affairs staff are aware of the goals and objectives of the LLC. This awareness can help to confirm that LLC goals and objectives are connected to broader divisional plans, which can ensure proper resourcing of the initiatives. Even on the same campus, there can be variation in the extent to which student affairs administration is connected to the LLCs. The director of residence life and assistant dean of students at St. Anselm described three different models of collaboration on St. Anselm's campus – an honors LLC that is driven primarily by the honors program and supported by residence life and student affairs, a residency class that is administered primarily as a partnership between faculty and residence life, and a learning community structure proposed by students based on their interests, supported by a faculty advisor, and assisted by residence life for programming and funding. This student-driven model serves as an example of how student affairs can be aware and supportive of LLC efforts, but not be active in shaping specific outcomes of the community. At St. Anselm, students in the learning community structure are provided with funding for programming in the community, but the organization of the community and the programming for the community are largely student-driven. There are programming expectations attached to being a designated learning community, which students must plan for in their application, but the execution of these programs, while supported by student affairs, is largely up to the students.

At the intermediate level, student affairs personnel are aware of the LLC and they provide targeted outreach in support of the LLC's goals and objectives. The Messina advisory board provides such outreach, helping to ensure that student affairs personnel are aware of the LLC and providing outreach when warranted. The board comprised the dean of undergraduate studies, the director of residence life, the dean of students, a representative from the Student Government Association, a representative from the Evergreens [orientation], representatives from each of the academic colleges who are all faculty members – some teaching in Messina, some not – and a representative from the Center for Community, Service and Justice. Because of these connections to the LLC, when big policy changes happen, there is typically some consideration for how the changes would affect the Messina community. The advisory board helped to navigate the effects on the Messina community when the campus began to move to a residential curriculum and having representatives from across campus was helpful to think through the various elements, even if each entity was not charged with implementing the curriculum.

At the advanced level, student affairs staff provide designated, specific, and ongoing support to the LLCs. As mentioned in the previous section, Elon University offers an example of how student affairs can be structured to work in sustained partnership with LLCs. Two positions on the campus facilitate this partnership, namely, the associate director of residence life for residential education and community development and the director of academic initiatives for the residential campus. Like most campuses that focus attention toward LLCs, the associate director of residence life reports to the director of residence life. However, at Elon, the associate director of residence life also reports to the director of academic initiatives, which is a position in the provost's office. This dual report structure helps to ensure that the associate director of residence life maintains focus on LLCs even when there are other pressing issues in the residence halls. The associate director of residence life at Elon shared how working in the dual report structure worked, explaining that "it adds another layer of expectation regarding how the relationship is supposed to work…and provides an expectation of what the relationship [between the LLCs and residence life] was supposed to look like." She described her partnership with Academic Affairs as a process of tag teaming and keeping each other in the loop so that "things are streamlined through both student life and academic affairs."

The director of academic initiatives for the residential campus agreed with this assessment, explaining that, although the dual structure works, it takes some awareness of different university organizational structures and what they mean to work effectively across Academic and Student Affairs. She explained that while Elon has "low fences" in terms of the siloes that exist at the institution, Student Life and Academic Affairs have different cultures, with Student Life having a much more hierarchical structure. In cultivating partnerships across these two entities, it has been important for her and others in Academic Affairs to be aware of these differences so that they do not inadvertently burn bridges by violating the hierarchical communication and working patterns in residence and student life, which would potentially erode trust and strain relationships. Although both serve on the Residential Living Learning Community Advisory Council and supervise the LLC advisors, their roles are differentiated, with the associate director of residence life overseeing budget and operations aspects and director of academic initiatives for the residential campus working on issues such as academic advising and curricular dimensions of the communities. It was clear in our conversation that both saw value in each other's position and indicated that because of their collaborative work, they provided better support to the LLCs.

Faculty

LLCs flourish when faculty are deeply involved in the life of the community. At their most foundational level, LLCs should have faculty who are formally affiliated with the LLC and participate in activities with LLC students. Residency Classes, which are one of the three LLC types on St. Anselm's campus, fit the foundational designation. In Residency Classes, a faculty member teaches a class in the residence hall for students who are living there. For example, one Residency Class was a drawing class; in addition to the course being taught in the hall, a common area in the hall served as a place where students stored all of their art supplies and artwork was displayed for other members of the residence hall to see.

At the intermediate level, faculty affiliates participate in planning and administering the academic elements of the LLC. Bucknell's LLCs fit this designation, as the faculty involved teach a first-year seminar. In addition, these faculty work in conjunction with an upper-class student, called a "junior fellow" to organize a "common hour," during which they engage in cocurricular activities including field trips, outings to campus events, dinners, and other activities.

Another example of intermediate faculty involvement can be found in several of the LLCs at Rider University. Faculty affiliated with their science LLC plan programs for students, including field trips to take samples on the beach and visiting a quarry to study rocks. In addition to these field trips, faculty participate in social activities with students, including a barbecue and annual kickball game. These activities help the faculty to shape the outcomes of the LLC and also build relationships with students that extend beyond the classroom.

At the advanced level, faculty live in residence with the students and engage in ongoing academic and social programmatic efforts. Many residential colleges fit the designation of advanced faculty participation by virtue of their structure. Hereford Residential College at the University of Virginia provides an illustration of this advanced level. The principal of Hereford lives in the college, working alongside the director of studies and program coordinator to oversee the day-to-day operations of the residential college. Collectively, they work alongside students to provide academic and cocurricular programming for the community.

Another example of the advanced level of faculty involvement can be found at Elon University, where faculty are integrated into LLCs in various capacities, one of which is to live on campus and help to support the community alongside residence life staff. The faculty-in-residence are charged with providing programming to students as well as engaging with them informally. The structure aims to ensure faculty and students have meaningful interactions so that students see them as approachable.

Academic Affairs Administration

We would be remiss if we did not acknowledge the important role that Academic Affairs administration plays in the development and operation of LLCs. If not for a willingness on the part of Academic Affairs to support LLC initiatives, it is exceedingly difficult to maintain them. At the foundational level, Academic Affairs provides support for LLC initiatives at the departmental, school, or provost level. This support might be enacted in the form of supporting a course release or extra compensation for faculty who are participating in an LLC. The faculty involved in Rider's LLCs, for example, are compensated by the dean of their college with support from the provost's office, but there is not a systematic process for ensuring that faculty are afforded these resources. Many LLCs with foundational support from Academic Affairs are likely to fulfill needs unsystematically as opportunities arise, as opposed to creating a structure for remuneration of faculty involved in LLC initiatives. Rider convened a task force to bolster the quality and sustainability of LLCs on campus, and among their recommendations was to look holistically at the compensation and support structure for faculty involved in these initiatives.

At the intermediate level, Academic Affairs ensures that LLC responsibilities are assigned formally and serve as one element of an academic administrator's role. Bucknell's Residential College Program (RCP) serves as an example of the intermediate level. The program is administered by a full-time program coordinator from Academic Affairs and a half-time operations specialist. These administrators recruit the faculty who support the RCP, each of whom is given a course release or $6,000 for their participation. Having support from Academic Affairs did not ensure collaboration between RLH, student, and Academic Affairs (another important aspect of the foundation, which we review in the next section); in fact, in the current RCP structure, RLH has little to nothing to do with programming, and it is not uncommon for live-in RLH staff to be unaware of the names or faces of the faculty teaching the seminars.

At the advanced level, Academic Affairs designates a professional staff member to lead academic/residential initiatives in partnership with residence life/student affairs. The Elon University structure we highlighted earlier provides an example of the advanced level of Academic Affairs administration. The position, director of academic initiatives for the residential campus, was created to ensure sustainability of the rapidly growing residential campus and faculty fellows program. When it was initially conceived, the position held a dual report to the provost's office and student life, but as time went on, the position was shifted to reside solely with the provost's office. Among the responsibilities of the position are to ensure that academic initiatives were developed and incorporated into Elon's eight residential neighborhoods. The position works in conjunction with residence life to recruit faculty and staff to serve in the residence halls in a range of roles, including LLC advisors and live-in positions.

As illustrated in the LLC typology (see Figure 3.2), in order to build a sustainable infrastructure for LLCs, personnel in various positions should be aware of the goals of the LLC, onboarded appropriately to support the LLC, and provided with adequate support from the university in order to sustain their involvement. In addition to personnel, it is important to consider whether funding is adequate to ensure viability and sustainability of LLC initiatives, which is the dimension of the infrastructure we address next.

Funding

The funding of LLCs varies greatly, both in terms of how the budget is allocated and what is included as part of the budget (Inkelas et al., 2018). As LLCs are initiated, it is important to consider the expenses associated with these communities and whether and how these expenses are allocated in a sustainable way.

Budget

At the foundational level, the budgets of RLH and Academic Affairs are not specifically designated for LLC use, but rather are used to advance goals and objectives when opportunities arise. At California Polytechnic Institute, funding for LLCs was drawn primarily from housing. Although the academic colleges were involved and supportive, they provided release time for faculty as opposed to actual funding. The associate director of the residential student experience explained,

> I know [the LLC] was a lot of money, and, and [the college] didn't necessarily have the money, but the Dean was like we're going to make it work, because we know this is huge and it's just grown from there....

BEST PRACTICES IN LIVING-LEARNING COMMUNITIES: INFRASTRUCTURE

As time went on, funding for the initiative grew because of support from the university president and an investment by the student government. So, whereas the institution started at the foundational level, they advanced to the intermediate level as time went on because of an institutional commitment to the program.

At the intermediate level, RLH and Academic Affairs budgets have designated LLC budget lines, but administer funds separately to support the goals and objectives of the LLC. Rider's LLCs operate with parallel budgets, with residence life bringing a programming budget into the mix, and student government bolstering the budget with additional programmatic funds. When the LLCs were created at Rider, the process of requesting a budget from student government was initiated by faculty, but over time residence life took over the process of soliciting the funds and helping to manage the student government side of the budget. The shift was made in recognition of the fact that residence life was much more accustomed to the university funding structure, costs associated with programs, and budget administration. Having the two designated funding sources means that when one department is targeted for budget cuts, as was the case a few years ago in residence life, funding from the other source can help to sustain the LLC.

At the advanced level, RLH and Academic Affairs either have a shared budget when possible or independent budgets that are co-administered to support the goals and objectives of the LLC. This co-administration or shared budget structure ensures that the needs of various aspects of the community – academic, social, and administrative – are all considered when spending decisions are made. Typically, LLCs that reach the advanced level of budget have made an institutional commitment to these communities and integrated them deeply into their planning. We have seen this sense of commitment from institutions and communities highlighted previously, including Elon and Hereford Residential College.

Expenses Included in the Budget

In addition to attending to the funding needs of the LLC, it is important to think about what expenses are included in the budget. At the foundational level, these expenses might include items that will result in sufficient support from administrators, faculty, and peers – salaries of administrators and student staff and stipends to encourage faculty involvement. In addition, at the foundational level, there should be a budget for programming to ensure that members of the LLC can engage in activities relevant to the community.

At the intermediate level, the expenses for the foundational level are included, and in addition, there will likely be items budgeted like food and catering, transportation, and assessment. These added line items will ensure that students are able to engage in activities relevant to the community, get outside the LLC into the greater community, and regularly examine the impact of the community on students' growth and development. St. Anselm's communities provide an example of this intermediate level. Residence life often helps to facilitate these budgeted items — ordering a bus when needed for a field trip, working to get lunch catered. Often faculty are outside of their wheelhouse when attending to these logistics, so residence life steps in to help, ensuring that the programs can happen in a seamless manner and faculty can focus on students' learning needs.

At the advanced level, additional budget items may include rent and parking subsidies for live-in faculty, meal plans for faculty and staff, professional development funds for faculty and staff involved in the community, and branding expenses to ensure the LLC is recognizable across campus. Messina community at Loyola University Maryland has found ways to include these extra budget items. When the program was established, funding was initially cobbled from other communities that had been sunsetted. However, once established, fundraising commenced with an external donor providing some funding and an internal grant competition providing the rest. As a result, students don't pay anything extra to be part of the community, and many of the supports integrated into the community are incentivized through the budget. For example, peer leaders receive a partial meal stipend for their participation in the community, and administrators and mentors are paid for their involvement, as are advisors. Excursions into Baltimore are also covered, and faculty and peer mentors are provided with budgets to ensure robust programming occurs.

GOALS AND OBJECTIVES

Listing the goals and objectives last in the typology of the infrastructure is not a reflection of their lack of importance, rather an indication that they often span each layer to the pinnacle. When we sought feedback on the revised model, one of the frequent comments made about the goals and objectives was the importance of depicting elements that might be unique to either Academic Affairs or RLH while also continuing to emphasize the symbiosis created when collaboration in goals and objectives occurs. The revised model honors the reality that goals and objectives exist at the foundation of every LLC and become more collaborative as the LLC becomes more integrated. Thus, at the foundational level, these goals and objectives are created within the silos of Academic Affairs and RLH, without much consideration for the others' goals and objectives. These entities work to enact these goals and objectives independently, but in parallel. One of the communities we talked to provided a foundational example. The program is housed in the provost's office, with limited connection to RLH. The provost's office has some shared goals and objectives across the residential colleges on campus, and each residential college has some unique goals and objectives as well. Our interviewee described the program as "heavy academic affairs funding, heavy academic affairs leadership, heavy academic focused curricular" and explained that they partner with residence life and other areas of student affairs for cocurricular learning. They do not sit down with residence life to plan or create shared goals or objectives. Rather, they are running parallel programs.

At the intermediate level, departmental goals and objectives are still developed independently, but each area is aware of the other's goals and objectives regarding the LLC and is supportive of the other in achieving them. Furthermore, the goals and objectives are measured and assessed regularly. The Gemstone Community at the University of Maryland serves as an intermediate example. Gemstone is a four-year, interdisciplinary honors program that emphasizes research and mentorship. Especially in students' first year of the program, when students are living together and engaging in shared coursework, Residence Life & Housing and Academic Affairs have a shared goal of enhancing students' first year on campus. For Academic Affairs, this goal means that courses have a transition and development dimension to them. For RLH, the emphasis is more on students' social integration. As students progress through the program, they may no longer live on campus because of limited options; however, often they still choose to live together. Ideally, they will begin to enact the community-building skills they learned while in the LLC (Jessup-Anger et al., 2019), but the goals and objectives that RLH initially set no longer pertain to them.

At the advanced level, goals and objectives are no longer created in isolation; rather, Academic Affairs and RLH develop and implement shared goals and objectives. Like the intermediate level, these goals and objectives are measured and assessed regularly. The LLCs at California Polytechnic Institute (Cal Poly) provide a clear example of how goals and objectives can evolve into an advanced form. Although initiated by residence life, preliminary conversations about the development of LLCs with deans, department chairs, and faculty wrestled with questions including "What are things that you wish students knew before they walked into the classroom?" and "What are the things in those first few weeks of school that you want reinforced during midterms?" Answering the preliminary questions enabled Academic Affairs to see the potential power in partnering with RLH. After these initial meetings, shared learning outcomes were developed as was an assessment plan. Associate deans and faculty engaged with RLH to set the goals and objectives, which helped with buy-in for the program and also the assessment.

CONCLUSION

When taken as a whole, the base layer of the revised BPM emphasizes establishing sufficient resources for the community and ensuring that goals and objectives are established for the community. Without establishing adequate resources in physical space, personnel, and funding for the community, sustainability of the LLC will be hampered. In addition, without clarifying the goals and objectives of the LLC, assessment will be impossible to design, and measuring effectiveness elusive, which will likely make the community prone to budget cuts when funding is tight. The Infrastructure Typology (Figure 3.2) offers a way for LLC administrators to initiate conversations about LLCs or examine their existing resources. As readers peruse the typology, some questions to ask include the following:

1. In which dimensions of resources is your LLC strong?
2. How might you prioritize improvements to resources?
3. If goals and objectives of Residence Life & Housing and Academic Affairs are not integrated, how might you start the discussions to align them more?

Attribute	Foundational	Intermediate	Advanced
Resources - Physical Space			
Residence hall rooms	Students are assigned to the same residence hall	Students are assigned to the same cluster or floor of rooms	Students are assigned to the same cluster or floor of rooms, which is branded appropriately for the LLC
LLC faculty space	Space can be reserved for LLC faculty use	LLC faculty have designated office space in the residence hall	LLC faculty live in the residence hall or on the premises in spaces designed for families
LLC staff space Note: LLC staff in this instance is not the same as residence life staff, who are assumed to already have workspace in the hall	Space can be reserved for LLC staff use	LLC staff have designated office space in the residence hall	LLC staff use designated office space for regular meetings with faculty and students in the community
Residence hall academic space	Space within the residence hall can be used for academic purposes	Classroom space designated for priority use by LLC	Designated and branded classroom space for LLC
Residence hall common space	Common space is available for LLC use	Common space is designated for priority use by LLC	Common space is designated and branded for LLC
Resources - Personnel			
Residence life staff in building	Hall director understands and supports LLC goals and objectives	Hall director works with hall staff to connect initiatives to LLC theme	Hall director and staff collaborate with LLC faculty to achieve goals and objectives

Figure 3.2 Infrastructure Typology.

Resident assistant student staff	Resident assistant understands and supports LLC goals and objectives	Resident assistant works to connect initiatives to LLC theme	Resident assistant collaborates with LLC faculty to achieve goals and objectives
Student staff Note: non-RA student LLC staff should be compensated at rates commensurate with their duties	Student staff (tutors, peer advisors) provide support as they would for other students	Designated, live-out peer mentors who support the LLC goals and objectives	Designated, live-in peer mentors who support the LLC goals and objectives both in the hall and in the classroom
Residence life administration	Professional staff support LLC initiatives through housing assignments	LLC responsibilities assigned formally as one element of a mid-level residence life position	Campus-wide LLC residential responsibilities designated as a primary aspect of professional staff role
Student affairs administration	Student affairs staff are aware of the goals and objectives of the LLC	Students affairs staff provide targeted outreach to LLC in support of goals and objectives	Student affairs staff provide designated, specific, and ongoing support to LLC
Faculty	Faculty are formally affiliated with the LLC and participate in activities with LLC students	Faculty affiliates participate in planning and administering the academic elements of the LLC	Faculty live in residence with the students and engage in ongoing academic and social programmatic efforts
Academic affairs administration	Departmental/School/Provost-level support for LLC initiatives	LLC responsibilities assigned formally as one element of an academic administrator's role	Provost office professional staff member leads academic/residential initiatives in partnership with residence life/student affairs

Figure 3.2 Continued

Resources - Funding				
Budget	Residence life and academic affairs budgets are not designated for LLC specifically but are used to advance goals and objectives when opportunities arise	Residence life and academic affairs budgets have designated LLC budget lines, but administer funds separately to support the goals and objectives of the LLC	Residence life and academic affairs either have a shared budget when possible or independent budgets that are co-administered to support the goals and objectives of the LLC
Expenses included as part of budget	Salaries of administrative & student staff Stipends for faculty Programming budget	Food & catering budget Transportation budget Assessment budget	Rent & parking subsidies for live-in faculty Meal plans for faculty & staff Professional development funds for staff & faculty Branding expenses
Goals and Objectives				
Context in which goals and objectives are set	Academic affairs and residence life & housing each has goals and objectives regarding the LLC and work to enact these in parallel with the other	Academic affairs and residence life & housing are aware of each other's goals and objectives regarding the LLC and supportive of the other in achieving them Goals & objectives are measurable and assessed	Academic affairs and residence life & housing develop and implement shared LLC goals and objectives

Figure 3.2 Continued

REFERENCES

Cox, B. E., & Orehovec, E. (2007). Faculty-student interaction outside the classroom: A typology from a residential college. *Review of Higher Education, 30*, 343–362.

Golde, C. M., & Pribbenow, D. A. (2000). Understanding faculty involvement in residential learning communities. *Journal of College Student Development, 41*(1), 27–40.

Inkelas, K. K., Jessup-Anger, J., Benjamin, M., & Wawrzynski, M. (2018). *Living-learning communities that work: A research-based model for design, delivery, and assessment*. Sterling, VA: Stylus Publishing, LLC.

Jessup-Anger, J. E., Armstrong, M., Kerrick, E., & Siddiqui, N. (2019). Exploring students' perceptions of their experiences in a social justice living-learning community. *Journal of Student Affairs Research and Practice, 56*(2), 194–206.

Jessup-Anger, J. E., & Benjamin, M. (2023). Engaging students in LLCs. In L. Lomicka & J. Eidum (Eds.), *The faculty factor: Developing faculty engagement with living learning communities* (pp. 164–179). Sterling, VA: Routledge.

Jessup-Anger, J. E., & Howell, C. (2021). All are welcome except you: Isolation in a social justice community. *Journal of College Student Development, 62*(2), 242–247.

Lyman Briggs website. (n.d.). Retrieved from https://lbc.msu.edu/about/index.htm

Sriram, R., Haynes, C., Weintraub, S. D., Cheatle, J., Marquart, C. P., & Murray, J. L. (2020). Student demographics and experiences of deeper life interactions within residential learning communities. *Learning Communities Research and Practice, 8*(1), Article 8.

Strange, C. C., & Banning, J. H. (2015). *Designing for learning: Creating campus environments for student success*. San Francisco, CA: Jossey-Bass.

Wawrzynski, M. R., & Jessup-Anger, J. E. (2010). From expectations to experiences: Using a structural typology to understand first-year student outcomes in academically-based living-learning environments. *Journal of College Student Development, 51*, 201–217.

Chapter 4

Best Practices in Living-Learning Communities: Climate

Socio-personal climates are intangible entities that are difficult to articulate physically but have an extensive effect on the environments they embody. For example, imagine two different universities with football teams in the same conference. One university, perennial favorites to win the conference every year, has a loyal fan base, including alumni from around the country and the world. The other university struggles to mount a winning season each year and doesn't have enough fans in its base to fill its stadium, despite giving away tickets for free. Now imagine the atmosphere on their respective campuses on a game day. Picture the tailgates and the stadiums, the sights and the sounds, the levels of excitement in the air. They are completely different, correct? On paper, they appear to be very similar: both universities have football teams, they play in the same conference, and they play their games on the same day and time of the week. However, the ambiances of the game days are completely different. Those differences are related to the climate.

Petersen and Spencer (1990), when distinguishing between academic cultures and climates, defined an academic climate as "the current common patterns of important dimensions of organizational life or its members' perceptions of and attitudes toward those dimensions" (p. 7). As opposed to cultures, the authors asserted that climates are "more concerned with current perceptions and attitudes rather than deeply held meanings, beliefs, and values" (p. 7). They went on to further define climates as having perceived and psychological, or felt, dimensions: the perceived climate relates to how individuals observe the organization's functions, and the psychological/felt climate concerns how individuals feel about their organization.

In early operationalizations of the academic and social climate in living-learning communities (LLC), the National Study of Living-Learning Programs (NSLLP) included both perceived and psychological elements in their descriptions of the residence hall climate in LLCs (Inkelas & Associates, 2007). The NSLLP composite measure representing the academic climate in residence halls included students' observations that stakeholders within the LLC created environments that were facilitative of academic success. Variables measured included noticing that students in their LLC studied a lot, or that the staff was helpful with academics. The academic climate measure also incorporated LLC students' feelings, such as the environment being, overall, supportive of academic achievement. Similarly, the residence hall social climate composite measure included both types of constructs: there were perceptual variables such as noting that students from different backgrounds interacted frequently with one another, as well as psychological/felt dimensions like the environment being appreciative of different races/ethnicities, or that students in the residence hall helped and supported one another.

In the original LLC Best Practices Model (Inkelas et al., 2018), academically and socially supportive climates were included as part of the "Academic Environment" tier of the model. Although we found the LLC climate to be important enough to be included in the original model, labeling it as part of the Academic Environment was somewhat of a misalignment, especially since the other elements of the level included more traditionally academic components such as courses for credit and faculty advising, which are much more objective and tangible aspects of an LLC. Early adopters of the Best Practices Model questioned why the LLC climate was listed as part of the Academic Environment in the model, both because some felt that climates are largely perceptual and not programmatic and thus did not match with the other blocks on the level, and because some felt that a healthy LLC climate was so central to the effectiveness of their communities that climates should be given a more prominent placement in the model.

There is empirical justification for LLC climates to have a more central position in a best practices model: research on the impact of college on students has consistently shown that students' perceptions of their peers' influence had a stronger impact on their outcomes than most other aspects of students' college experiences – including their curriculum, faculty interactions, and institutional policies (Astin, 1993). And, although an LLC climate can be shaped by other elements than peer influence (e.g., faculty engagement, staff involvement, physical layout of the building), it is the peer-to-peer interaction that is most strongly associated with the residence hall climate. In a similar vein, the original LLC Best Practices Model tended to foreground LLC programs, events, and activities, especially with the bulk of the model focusing on "Academic" and "Cocurricular" environments such as courses for credit, faculty advising, study groups, and theme-related activities. This emphasis tended to spotlight the *what* of LLCs over the *who*, and in the process, under-acknowledged the key roles that students themselves play in the life of an LLC.

Accordingly, in the revised Best Practices Model (see Figure 4.1), LLC climates occupy a much more prominent position as its own layer of the pyramid. The climate level rests directly atop the Infrastructure level, in that – like in Maslow's theory – an actual LLC could not exist without its basic needs of goals

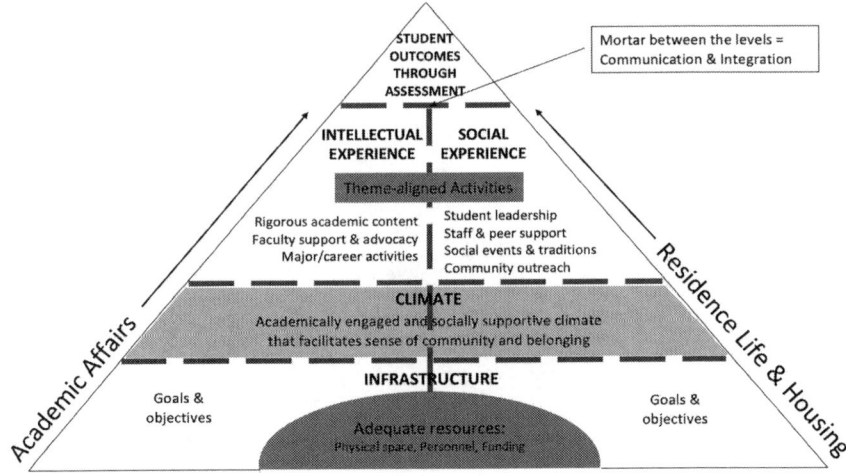

Figure 4.1 The Climate of the Revised Best Practices Model.

and objectives and adequate resources vis-à-vis a Residence Life & Housing and Academic Affairs partnership. Moreover, the influences of Residence Life & Housing and the Academic Affairs unit still permeate the climate layer; these two entities not only contribute tangibly to the infrastructure layer, but their policies and practices affect participants' perceptions and observations about their LLC. However, the LLC climate also serves as a foundation for the Intellectual and Social Experiences level of the model that lies above it, in deference to the peer influence and perception of support within the climate that determines whether students will engage in academic and social programming in the first place. In other words, if students participating in an LLC do not feel as though there is a climate within the community that supports and encourages them to engage with the programming and one another, they will not participate in the programming – no matter the quality and quantity of the programming offered.

Consistent with the original LLC Best Practices Model, the climate is distinguished into academic and social components, but they are now described as climates that (a) academically engage students; and (b) socially support students. Moreover, we have added a third component: environments that facilitate a sense of belonging. It is important to underscore that the academic and social climates of an LLC do not relate to actual programs, activities, or events that LLCs develop and execute, but instead concern the general atmosphere and conditions that underlie the community that either enable or inhibit successful programs, activities, and events.

ACADEMICALLY ENGAGED COMMUNITY

Effective LLCs should stimulate students to participate in academic endeavors related to their themes. LLCs can create a plethora of programming for their students, but if few-to-no students participate in them, then the programming cannot attain the desired effects. Thus, student participation in an LLC's programs and events forms a critical basis for its academic climate. At a foundational level, at least some students need to participate in the LLC's program offerings, and typically, it is often the same core sub-set of students who participate. At a more intermediate level, the LLC is able to engage the majority of its members to participate in its program offerings on a regular basis. At its most advanced or optimal level, almost all or all of the LLC participants engage regularly with the programming. Further, at the advanced level, students are often actively involved in the development of the programs, and seek to keep involvement levels high by having "veteran" LLC members engage with "newcomers" to ensure participation.

One way to build the expectation of engagement while also capitalizing on LLC student "veterans" is to conduct a retreat or workshop prior to the start of the fall semester. The Gemstone Program at the University of Maryland runs a 2-day retreat before the beginning of the fall semester, which approximately two-thirds of the incoming first-year students attend. Former Gemstone participants are the camp leaders, who engage the new students in an assortment of team activities, including breaking them into smaller groups based on the floor where the students will be living on campus. Thus, by the time the students arrive on campus, they already know many of the other Gemstone students and are ready to engage with the fall programming.

Avenues for generating new ideas for academic programs, activities, and events in an LLC are essential for its success. Although some highly successful programs can and should be continued – and even become traditions – within a community, LLCs cannot rely on the same set of academic programs year-after-year. In order to stay relevant and vibrant, LLCs must be willing to wrestle with and enact new ideas. In healthy LLCs, the introduction of these new ideas should come from anyone in the community, including faculty, staff, and student members. At a foundational level, new ideas to deepen the intellectual engagement of an LLC should regularly flow from its faculty and staff, but sometimes, new ideas could come from student participants. At the intermediate level, faculty, staff, and students in the LLC regularly engage with one another on novel intellectual ideas, and at the most advanced level, robust and innovative ideas originate equally and spontaneously from students, staff, and faculty.

Ashby College at the University of North Carolina – Greensboro inspires its residential college students to participate in cocurricular activities and events inside and outside of the colleges by linking the social justice curriculum of the course the students take with cocurricular opportunities around campus. The instructor of the social justice class also coordinates with the Residence Hall Council's Social Justice Committee, so there is strong cross-over between students in the course and participation in discussions about current events that the Hall Council sponsors. The course also involves a significant amount of writing and reflection, especially around difference. Students are encouraged to reflect on how they might see something differently or do something differently as a result of what they learned in the course.

Part of an LLC's ability to generate new intellectual ideas relates to its willingness to experiment and try new things. Particularly with more stable LLCs that have been in existence for a while, stagnation can set in and the community can begin to "rest on its laurels" by putting on the same programs year-after-year. Yet, strong LLC themes, goals, and objectives should be flexible enough to grow and change over time. Thus, existing programming can be re-invented occasionally, and new programming should be introduced. Foundationally, LLC stakeholders may encounter some resistance to break with or revise certain traditions, but there should be an occasional interest in trying new things and ways of operating at a basic level. Similarly, as if on a continuum, LLCs at an intermediate level are working to become the type of community where new ideas and ways of operation are constantly evolving and being tried. Finally, at its most advanced level, LLCs should be a place where it is commonplace for the community to try new ideas and ways of doing things, and thus embrace the belief that programming is ever-evolving and not stagnant.

The LLCs at California Polytechnic Institute keep their programming fresh and evolving by working with community partners. Much attention is paid to matching community organizations with the themes of the LLCs; for example, the Engineering LLC is paired with Habitat for Humanity (which focuses on building affordable homes) as its partner, and the College of Science LLC would be matched with a community partner focused on nature, such as a local creek clean-up effort. Programming would be developed around the needs of the community partners, and sometimes, the community partners would come to the campus. For example, the LLC matched with a Foster Youth program had youth they served come to Cal Poly to introduce them to college life and raise their efficacy regarding their potential to attend college. Working with community partners required the students, faculty, and staff in the LLCs to think creatively, be flexible, and consider an external stakeholder's point of view. In many ways, this partnership was evocative of Cal Poly's slogan: "learn by doing."

Change can be difficult, and offering new ideas – especially in an environment that has traditionally been effective – can be daunting. The expectations for engagement, encouragement of creativity, and openness to experimentation to keep engagement fresh addressed the potential for change in LLC programming. The final element of LLC academic climates relates to how stakeholders interact with one another around differing viewpoints. These viewpoints can involve the management of the LLC, or they can simply concern how individuals interact across differences. First, it is important to emphasize that there is no room for intolerance of differences by race/ethnicity, gender, culture, religion, family background, or nationality. As such, communities with such intolerant attitudes do not even rise to the foundational level in the Best Practices Model. Yet, other types of differing viewpoints, such as theoretical disagreements, political divides, and matters of taste or preference, can and should exist within a diverse LLC.

At a foundational level, effective LLCs should also have academic climates in which differing points of view are sought out and included in intellectual discussions. At the next or intermediate level, intellectual discussions should include differing viewpoints, with the acknowledgement that diverse views are to be tolerated. This may be more difficult than it seems at first blush: with social pressures to immediately demonstrate one's support for opinions that one feels are widely held by the majority of the group (i.e., virtue signaling), holding discussions with non-judgment may take practice and patience at first. Thus, at the most advanced level, intellectual discussions in the LLC can be spirited and dynamic, while also including different points of view and free from castigation or contempt. Indeed, because in an LLC these discussions often occur in the same location as where the students live, it is crucially important that intellectual discussions remain non-judgmental so that students can feel safe and at ease in their campus residences.

One LLC environment that creates the conditions that exemplify all of the aspects of an academically engaged community is the Gemstone research project at the University of Maryland. The Gemstone LLC, part of the Honors College, is a multidisciplinary four-year research program in which selected students design, conduct, and write about an independent research project under the guidance of a faculty mentor and the Gemstone staff. Many of the programs and events in Gemstone revolve around the students' research topics, which naturally facilitates student interest in attending the events. The students, staff, and faculty in the program regularly engage in robust conversations about the development of the students' research project, offering new ways to observe and interpret what the students are planning or finding. Moreover, as is often the case with research projects, some aspect of the design will inevitably not go according to plan, so students learn to be resilient and try a different approach, with the gentle encouragement of their faculty and staff mentors. Finally, through the deep study of their research topics, students learn that science is also evolving, with scholars often disagreeing about current interpretations of various phenomena. Yet, those disagreements, although sometimes spirited, are tolerated and even encouraged – as scientific knowledge can only move forward with the introduction and critique of new ideas.

SOCIALLY SUPPORTIVE COMMUNITY

It can sometimes be challenging to disentangle elements of an LLC's climate related to social support from elements characterizing academic engagement. Indeed, the challenge can be reminiscent of the "chicken or the egg" dilemma of which comes first: do students first need to have an open mind in order to be welcoming of difference, or do students first need to approach their communities with a sense of support and care in order to be able to accept difference with an open mind? Like the paradox itself, it is perhaps less important to know which relies on the other and instead embrace that we cannot have one without the other any longer. Accordingly, elements of a socially supportive LLC include the following characteristics: (a) they are welcoming, caring communities; (b) they are open to and accepting of social differences; and (c) they encourage (appropriate) risk-taking.

An almost axiomatic assertion is that an LLC should be a welcoming community, as opposed to an elitist or cliquish one. As was discussed previously, LLCs are students' homes while on campus, and while other portions of their collegiate lives might include debate or struggle or challenge, students should always feel as though they can be at ease in their homes. The level and depth of support students can receive in their LLCs differentiates the various levels of the typology. For example, as a foundation, the LLC community should comprise an atmosphere that is welcoming, where individuals are kind and pleasant to one another. At the next intermediate level, the atmosphere adds supportive peers to a welcoming environment. Peer support might include helping out a student with homework or pitching in to keep the community clean. At the most advanced level, the LLC community is welcoming, marked by peer support, and genuinely and proactively concerned for each other's well-being. This concern might involve inviting a shy hallmate to dinner in the dining hall, checking in on a student in the hall who hasn't been seen out of their room in a while, or even ensuring that a student in need of help gets to the resources they need.

LLC staff can model the kind of caring, welcoming community they wish to foster by offering their support to students. For example, the staff of the Sport Management and Media LLC at Elon University check-in sporadically with their first-year students during their fall semester transition. Even if the first-year students are not asking for help, the staff reaches out to reinforce that there are people in their LLC who care about them and are available to assist them should they need help. Moreover, after students have made the transition and know their LLC environments to be welcoming and supportive, they can then lean on their peers in the hall to "have their backs" when they need help. For example, when asked for instances when they knew their LLC hallmates were proactively concerned for their well-being, students at Hereford Residential College at the University of Virginia were quick to provide many illustrations, from finding a new phone charger cord slipped under their door after theirs broke to knowing that it would be okay to wake up a friend in the early morning hours to help "liberate" a large insect from their room because they were too frightened to do it themselves.

One of the greatest sources of learning opportunities for undergraduates on a residential campus is to be able to learn about different social identities through the backgrounds and experiences of their peers. These identities are more personally shared in residential spaces than most anywhere else on campus, whether they be personal artifacts displayed in students' rooms, favorite foods that arrive in care packages, or the age-old argument of whether carbonated beverages are called "soda" or "pop" or even "Coke." At a foundational level, diverse student social identities in an LLC should be acknowledged and tolerated instead of hidden and scorned. At an intermediate level, social identity differences can take the form of learning opportunities, where students can be introduced to new ideas of doing and seeing things that are appreciated and welcomed in the community. At its most advanced level, diverse social identities are woven into the fabric of the community; they are not seen as exotic or unusual, but instead treated as integral to the vibrance of the LLC.

In the introductory course in the Sport Management and Media LLC at Elon University, the instructor had her students construct individual social identity maps that consist of three nested rings: the outermost ring is used to describe aspects of one's given identity, or attributes that students had no choice in, such as their physical characteristics, number of siblings, age, etc. In the next ring, students would list aspects of their chosen identity, or attributes they pursued in their lives, like their major, their hobbies, their religious affiliation, etc. Finally, in the center ring, they would write about their core attributes, or enduring values, belief, skills, etc. that make them unique – curious, artistic, introverted. The students then shared their identity maps with the others in the class. In the process, the students learned about the ways in which they were similar to and distinct from the peers that they did not know previously. They also discovered connections that their peers observed between their given and chosen identities that they hadn't identified for themselves. And, gradually, their diverse social identities became an integral part of their community.

Finally, the social climate in an LLC should be one where students are encouraged to take risks, risk making mistakes, and given the space to learn from their mistakes free of judgment. Just as the academic climate of an LLC should be non-judgmental about opposing intellectual viewpoints, the social climate should be supportive enough that students feel comfortable to try new things, even if they do not know if they will be successful. To be clear, however, the

LLC environment should not be supportive of, or even worse coercive toward, risk-taking that is physically or mentally dangerous to individuals. The types of social risk-taking we are advocating relate to trying new experiences, learning new skills, and breaking out of old habits in ways that could help students grow, develop, and thrive.

At a foundational level, the LLC environment should be supportive of students being able to take risks and sometimes make mistakes. At the intermediate level, not only do students feel as though they can take risks and possibly make mistakes, but they also know that they will not be judged if they were to be unsuccessful or make a mistake. And, at the advanced level, risks are taken, mistakes are made, and the environment as a whole learns from the mistakes in a non-judgmental format that ultimately improves the experience for everyone.

The LLCs at Cal Poly used an opportunity presented by a university information campaign to invite their students to learn more about the Native American tribes associated with the names of new buildings on the campus. The buildings were named after local cities, but using the names of the cities used by area tribes in their tribal language. Moreover, because these tribal languages are gradually being lost, the information the students were learning about the tribes and their languages represented the preservation of the history and culture of the people who first inhabited the land on which the students were currently residing. No doubt, in the process, names, pronunciations, and spellings were mangled, and the potential for cultural misappropriations was probable. Yet, the temporary discomfort of making a mistake was far overshadowed by the opportunity to contribute to something greater than themselves.

FACILITATIVE OF SENSE OF BELONGING

Ultimately, a strong and supportive academic and social climate should lead students in those environments to feel supported and connected with others. This sense of support and connection undergirds a sense of belonging, which brings us back to Abraham Maslow! In his Hierarchy of Needs, Maslow's (1954/1987) third level was characterized by love and belongingness needs. Belongingness, he posited, referred to a human emotional need for interpersonal relationships, affiliating, connectedness, and being part of a group. In his hierarchy, Maslow argued that, after individuals satisfied their basic needs (air, food, shelter, sleep, etc.) and a sense of personal safety and security, the next level of human need is belongingness, which preceded the ability to achieve self-esteem and self-actualization. In college, students' sense of belonging has been associated with a myriad of important outcomes, including heightened academic achievement, stronger persistence, and improved mental health (Baumeister & Leary, 1995; Strayhorn, 2012; Yeager et al., 2016).

The role of LLCs in augmenting students' sense of belonging is significant for two reasons. First, undergraduate first-year retention has been significantly linked to sense of belonging (Barclay et al., 2018; Davis et al., 2019). Meanwhile, the majority of LLCs cater solely to first-year or first- and second-year students only. Thus, LLCs can provide students a sense of belonging that is beneficial to retention during the exact time when it is the most needed. Moreover, sense of belongingness to a sub-community within a larger university context has been shown to facilitate overall college success in a number of contexts, including commuter student extracurricular involvement (Manley Lima, 2014), racially/ethnically marginalized students (Museus & Maramba, 2011), and women students in computing (Sax et al., 2018). Indeed, using data from the NSLLP, Johnson et al. (2007) found that students' perceptions of their residential hall climate had strong and significant relationships to their sense of belonging.

Consequently, we have included the construct of sense of belonging in the Climate section of the revised Best Practices Model. We view the climate for a sense of belonging in LLCs to be related to four aspects: (a) sense of connection; (b) feeling of mattering; (c) atmosphere of mutual trust; and (d) sense of home. Similar to the feeling of having a welcoming community, we view students' sense of connection to their LLC as a scaffolded relationship. At a foundational level, students (and faculty and staff) should at least feel a connection to their LLC community. At the intermediate level, they should feel a deeper connection, or bond, to the community. Finally, at the advanced level, that bond with their LLC community should extend to actively helping others to feel connected as well.

Although they are symbolic, visual indicators that unite the LLC can be important in creating a shared sense of connection. Thus, it is beneficial for LLCs to create their own logos, brand their own colors, or even identify mascots or mottos. In addition, LLC swag such as t-shirts, stickers, water bottles, tote bags, and graduation cords using the logos, colors, mascots, and mottos help the students, faculty, and staff of the LLCs to feel a bond with one another. Indeed, even after the student is no longer participating in the LLC, every time they see that LLC's t-shirt on a student walking down the sidewalk, or its sticker on the laptop of the person studying across from them in the library, it will summon the common bond they feel with the program and the people in it.

In Ashby Residential College at the University of North Carolina – Greensboro, the owl is the college symbol and is used on everything from t-shirts to coffee mugs to lip balm. A banner over the building's entry welcomes LLC members and visitors to the residential college, and branded umbrellas over outdoor tables remind all that they are at Ashby. The various "swag" used is designed by students, further investing them in the identity of the LLC.

More than merely connecting with their communities, effective LLC environments should facilitate in students that they matter. Schlossberg (1989) defined mattering as students' need to feel that their presence on campus was noticed and important to others. Accordingly, at a foundational level, students should feel as though they matter to the various stakeholders (faculty, staff, and peers) in their LLC communities. At the next higher level, students not only feel as though they matter but can also contribute to others' sense of mattering. And, at the advanced level, that sense of mattering transfers to their feelings about not only the LLC but also the institution-at-large.

Several of the LLCs at Cal Poly pre-establish student study groups by discipline. They also use table tents identifying what someone was studying in a common room so others who might need help with that subject or were studying the same subject could join them. While this is a simple mechanism, the underlying message that the students absorb is that their LLC is a place where peers care about their academic success and are willing to help one another – that they matter.

Students' sense of mattering and belonging is based, in some part, on their level of trust with others in their community. Trust, consequently, forms the basis of students' willingness to engage with others and with programming – especially if it involves doing something outside of their initial level of comfort. At the foundational level, students should feel as though they can trust the faculty, staff, and students in their LLC. Once students establish that sense of trust, at the intermediate level, they can spread that sentiment to others in the LLC by working to create an environment of trust with everyone. Finally, at the advanced level, the level of trust they feel in their LLC allows students to be more trusting of the university-at-large and more fully engage in their experiences outside of the LLC as well.

The faculty fellows of the residential colleges at Bucknell University take turns inviting their students to their homes for dinner. In their faculty fellows' homes, students are introduced to the fellows' families, pets, treasured keepsakes, and favorite foods. The fellows' dinner program is a mechanism for creating stronger LLC communities at Bucknell, but they also serve the purpose of allowing students to see the personal lives of their faculty, to find commonalities with them, and to begin to recognize faculty as regular people. The dinners must, then, serve to increase the level of trust between the students and their faculty in ways that meeting on campus, or even in the LLC residence hall, cannot.

Ultimately, a strong and healthy LLC academic and social climate that facilitates a sense of belonging within its students should enable students to think of their LLC with a sense of home. At the foundational level, students can feel as though their LLC is a "home base" on campus, and at a higher level, that home base is where they feel comfortable being themselves. And, at the highest level, that sense of home and comfort allows them to be at peace when in the LLC, and encourages them to help others in the LLC be at peace as well.

Located on the edge of the campus at the University of Virginia, Hereford Residential College is the residential complex located furthest away from the center of grounds. Although Hereford does not recruit or market itself as a diverse living environment, its resident composition is two-thirds students of color and approximately 20% international students. When the Hereford staff conducted focus groups on students' sense of belonging, the participants were asked why so many diverse students chose to live at Hereford. The popular response was that the support and kinship they found at Hereford, coupled with its distance from the rest of campus whose culture more closely mirrored a wealthy, White, and privileged enclave, helped them feel as though the residential college was an oasis — a place where they felt safe and comfortable, where they were not tokenized. In fact, some of the focus group participants from marginalized groups acknowledged that if it were not for the residential college community, they would not have any place at the university where they felt they belonged. Yet, because they had Hereford as their home base, they felt they could cope with whatever other academic and social stressors they faced in the other parts of the university.

CONCLUSION

As practitioners work to build and maintain effective LLCs and researchers endeavor to operationalize best practices for LLCs, we offer the following typology (see Figure 4.2) that outlines the various aspects of academically engaged communities, socially supportive communities, and communities that facilitate a sense of belonging within LLCs.

Reading through the typology below (regarding climate), consider the following questions about your own LLC:

1. What are the existing strengths and potential barriers your LLC faces when addressing the climate in your community?
2. What are the incentives for student participation in your LLC? What encourages students to participate in your LLC programming and community?
3. How can your LLC encourage students to be open-minded and supportive of one another?
4. What structural and interpersonal mechanisms can be put in place to facilitate a welcoming, inclusive, and inviting environment that fosters students' sense of belonging and connection?

Attribute	Foundational	Intermediate	Advanced
Academically Engaged Community			
Student participation in programs & events	Some (typically, the same core set) students participate in programs & events, more-or-less on regular basis	Majority of students participate in programs & events on regular basis	Programs & events are planned and well participated in by whole of the LLC community, and peers engage with newcomers to ensure participation
Intellectual curiosity & creativity in community	Occasional ideas for deepening intellectual engagement originating primarily by faculty & staff, and sometimes by students in LLC community	Regular engagement of intellectual ideas by faculty, staff & students in LLC community	Robust & innovative intellectual ideas originating equally from students, faculty & staff in LLC community
Willingness to experiment and try new things	Occasional interest in trying new things and ways of doing things; some resistance to breaking of traditions	Working to become a community where new ideas and ways of doing things are piloted and evolved	Commonplace for trying new ideas & ways of doing things; openness to evolving nature of programming, including traditions
Non-judgment of opposing views	Inclusion of differing viewpoints by members of LLC community in intellectual discussions	Intellectual discussions include different views by LLC community members, with acknowledgement that diverse views are to be tolerated	Spirited intellectual discussion, including different viewpoints, by members of LLC community without castigation or contempt
Socially Supportive Community			
Welcoming, caring community	LLC community atmosphere is welcoming	LLC community atmosphere is welcoming and supportive of peers	LLC community atmosphere is welcoming, kind, supportive of peers, and

Figure 4.2 Climate Typology.

			proactively concerned for each other's well-being
Openness to and acceptance of social differences	Diverse student social identities are acknowledged and tolerated in LLC community	Diverse student social identities are appreciated and welcomed in LLC community	Diverse student social identities are celebrated and an integral fabric of the LLC community
Encouragement of (appropriate) risk-taking	LLC environment is supportive of students taking risks and sometimes making mistakes	LLC environment is encouraging of risk-taking and non-judgmental when mistakes are made	LLC environment is energized by collective risk-taking, and lessons learned from mistakes are discussed non-judgmentally
Facilitative of Sense of Belonging			
Sense of connection	Students, faculty, and staff feel connected to the other members of the LLC community	Students, faculty, and staff feel a bond with other members of the LLC community	Students, faculty, and staff feel a bond with the community and actively help others feel identified with the LLC
Feeling of mattering	Students feel as though they matter to their faculty, staff, & peers in LLC community	Students feel as though they matter to the entire LLC community and help others to feel as though they matter too	Students feel as though they matter, not only to their LLC community but also to the institution by virtue of their participation in the LLC
Atmosphere of mutual trust	Students feel that they can trust the faculty, staff, and peers in their LLC community	Students feel that they can trust members of their LLC community, and work to create an environment of trust among their peers	Students feel that they can trust members of their LLC community, and that trust emboldens them to be more engaged with their college experience
Sense of home	Students feel as though their LLC is "home base" on campus	Students identify with their LLC as "home," and feel comfortable when there	Students identify with their LLC as "home," feel at peace when there, and mutually reinforce the feeling of home with others

Figure 4.2 Continued

REFERENCES

Astin, A. W. (1993). *What matters in college?: Four critical years revisited*. San Francisco, CA: Jossey-Bass.

Barclay, T. H., Barclay, R. D., Mimis, A., Sargent, Z., & Robertson, K. (2018). Academic retention: Predictors of college success. *Education, 139*(2), 59–70.

Baumeister, R. F., & Laery, M. R. (1995). The need to belong: Desire for interpersonal attachments and as fundamental human motivation. *Psychological Bulletin, 117*(3), 497–529.

Davis, G. M., Hanzsek-Brill, M. B., Petzold, M. C., & Robinson, D. H. (2019). Students' sense of belonging: The development of a predictive retention model. *Journal of the Scholarship of Teaching and Learning, 19*(1), 117–127.

Inkelas, K. K., & Associates. (2007). *The national study of living-learning programs: 2007 report of findings*. College Park, MD: The University of Maryland.

Inkelas, K. K., Jessup-Anger, J., Benjamin, M., & Wawrzynski, M. (2018). *Living-learning communities that work: A research-based model for design, delivery, and assessment*. Sterling, VA: Stylus Publishing, LLC.

Johnson, D. R., Soldner, M. E., Leonard, J., Alvarez, P., Inkelas, K. K., Rowan-Kenyon, H. T., & Longerbeam, S. D. (2007). Examining sense of belonging among first-year undergraduates from different racial/ethnic groups. *Journal of College Student Development, 48*(5), 525–542.

Manley Lima, M. C. (2014). *Commuter students' social integration: The relationship between involvement in extracurricular activities and sense of belonging*. [Doctoral dissertation, George Washington University]. ProQuest Dissertations and Theses database.

Maslow, A. (1954/1987). *Motivation and personality*. New York: Harper/Addison-Wesley.

Museus, S. D., & Maramba, D. C. (2011). The impact of culture on Filipino American students' sense of belonging. *The Review of Higher Education, 34*(2), 231–258.

Peterson, M. W., & Spencer, M. G. (1990). Understanding academic culture and climate. Assessing Academic Climates and Cultures. *New Directions for Institutional Research, 68*.

Sax, L. J., Blaney, J. M., Lehman, K. J., Rodriguez, S. L., George, K. L., & Zavala, C. (2018). Sense of belonging in computing: The role of introductory courses for women and underrepresented minority students. *Social Sciences, 7*(8), 122.

Schlossberg, N. K. (1989). Marginality and mattering: Key issues in building community. In D. C. Roberts (Ed.), *Designing campus activities to foster a sense of community* (New Directions for Student Services, No. 48, p. 115). San Francisco, CA: Jossey Bass.

Strayhorn, T. L. (2012). *College students' sense of belonging: A key to educational success for all students*. New York: Routledge.

Yeager, D. S., Walton, G. M., Brady, S. T., Akcinar, E. N., Paunesku, D., Keane, L., Kamentz, D., Ritter, G., Duckworth, A. L., Urstein, R., Gomez, E. M., Markus, H. R., Cohen, G. L., & Dweck, C. S. (2016). Teaching a lay theory before college narrows achievement gaps at scale. *Proceedings of the National Academy of Sciences, 113*, E3341–E3348.

Chapter 5

Best Practices in Living-Learning Communities: Intellectual Experience

As illustrated in Figure 5.1, in the revised Best Practices Model (BPM), intellectual and social experiences occupy the same level of the pyramid to illustrate the importance of both aspects in helping students achieve the goals and objectives of the community. Although primarily fostered by Academic Affairs (which is why it is on the left side of the pyramid), Residence Life & Housing also help to foster the intellectual experience by providing support for intellectual theme-related activities. The intellectual experience is what sets a living-learning community (LLC) apart from a theme floor or traditional residence hall floor. By virtue of housing students together, all residence halls offer students a social experience. The intellectual experience, in contrast, must be cultivated by introducing and integrating academic content into the living space. This cultivation is initiated at lower levels of the pyramid, when Academic Affairs, either alone or in conjunction with housing and residence life, sets goals and objectives that are intellectual in nature. Examples of these might be related to the development of students' academic success skills (e.g. as a result of participation in an LLC, students will report engaging with other students about class-related material on a weekly basis), or transition to college (e.g. as a result of participating in an LLC, students will report visiting a professor about academic matters outside of class several times throughout the year). The outcomes could also be focused on the development of content knowledge (e.g. "As a result of participation in an LLC, students will be able to apply computer science theory and software development fundamentals to produce computer-based solutions" [The College of New Jersey Science Learning Outcomes]). In addition to academic outcomes, the foundational level of the pyramid illustrates the importance of adequate resources meant to support academic endeavors, including physical space, personnel, and funding. Chapter 3 provides an overview of these resources. The intellectual experience is also predicated upon the creation of an academically engaged climate, which we discussed in Chapter 4. Without this engagement, students will not be primed to take advantage of the theme-aligned activities that make the intellectual experience rich and meaningful to students.

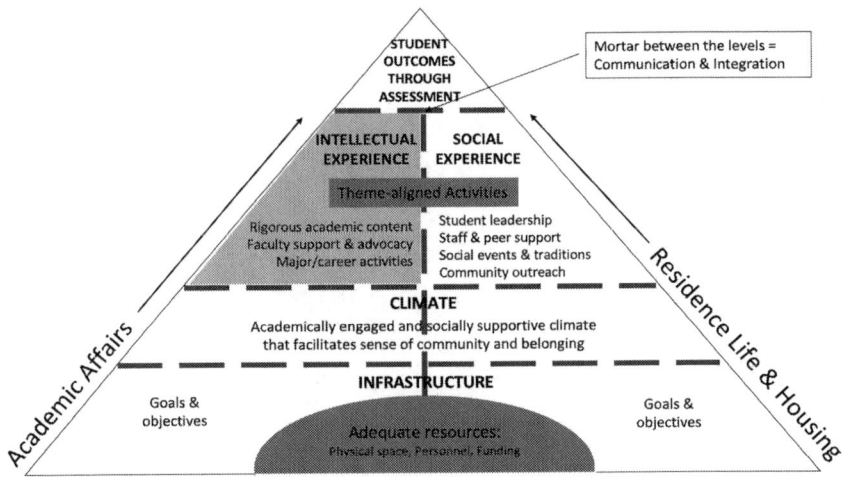

Figure 5.1 The Intellectual Experience of the Revised Best Practices Model.

Markers of a robust intellectual experience are found in the high-impact practice research literature. These experiences are often integrative, providing students with the opportunity to reflect on their learning, integrate it into their existing understanding, and apply it to real world scenarios (Kuh et al., 2017). In addition, a robust intellectual experience often includes high expectations for academic performance; significant time and effort on academic endeavors for a prolonged period; substantive interactions with faculty and peers about academic matters; engagement with diverse perspectives, circumstances, and demographics; and frequent, timely, and constructive feedback (Kuh, 2008; Kuh et al., 2013, 2017).

The Intellectual Experience in the revised BPM is less prescriptive than the Academic Environment Level was in the original model. Although we laud for-credit courses as something advanced LLCs should strive for, our discussions with LLC faculty and practitioners, as well as our own experience, taught us that intellectual content can take many forms and provide an anchor for the intellectual experience of an LLC. In addition, the revised model provides an expanded role for faculty in the LLC. Although faculty advising can establish a route to the development of meaningful faculty and student interactions, there are other mechanisms for developing these relationships as well. Jessup-Anger and Benjamin (2023) developed a model for deepening faculty and student relationships in LLCs that helps to advance understanding of faculty advocacy. As a precursor to faculty and student interaction in an LLC, the model encourages LLC administrators to identify faculty who might be a good fit to participate in the community. These faculty may be seeking meaningful relationships with students, desiring to engage in experimental pedagogy or interdisciplinary work with colleagues, or are wanting to replicate their own experiences at small liberal arts colleges. Once faculty become engaged in the LLC, they can become staunch advocates for the community by serving as teachers, administrators, champions, mentors, learners, and more. Often, these faculty champions work in conjunction with RLH and students to advance the aims of the community, which will enhance the intellectual offerings of the LLC, including study groups and major/career-related activities. Next we detail the specifics of each dimension of the intellectual experience, providing a typology illustrating foundational, intermediate, and advanced levels of each dimension and examples from our discussion with LLC administrators.

RIGOROUS ACADEMIC CONTENT

Academic content is what differentiates an LLC from other residential spaces, including traditional residence halls and theme/affinity houses. Defined as academically focused programming that aligns with the LLC theme, research illustrates the magic that can happen when learning and living are conjoined. When LLCs offer environments marked by academic challenge and high expectations, students lean in to the challenge, ultimately demonstrating a proclivity toward learning (Jessup-Anger, 2012; Wawrzynski et al., 2009) and a willingness to work with their peers to deepen their understanding (Jessup-Anger et al., 2020). At the foundational level, rigorous academic content can take the form of non-credit bearing courses, workshops, or discussion series organized by LLC administrators, faculty, or peers. In addition, this content may be shaped by guest lectures by university faculty who are invited into the community to provide their expertise on particular topics.

Several LLC administrators we spoke with described activities that would fall under the foundational classification, even if these communities also had intermediate and advanced content as well. In Hereford Residential College at the University of Virginia, for example, students have the opportunity to participate in a bi-weekly music meditation led by a music professor, during which they learn different kinds of meditation while listening to music selections. This activity aligns with the theme, *mindfulness,* which is one of three themes advanced by the community (the others being social awareness and sustainability). Another example comes from Bucknell's LLCs, which utilize an LLC "common hour," during which no classes are held, to bring in guest speakers to discuss topics common to the LLCs.

At the intermediate level, rigorous academic content becomes more formalized. It may take the form of a for-credit course offered by an academic department that is dovetailed with an LLC. Alternatively, it may be an LLC-sponsored service learning series that is coupled with a discussion meant to deepen students' experiences. Often first-year seminars or other required general education courses are ripe for partnering academic departments and LLCs. Since students take these courses as a group, they often deepen their relationships with one another and discuss their experiences outside of class. Elon's Sport Management and Media LLC offers perspective about the affordances and constraints of this approach. In our discussion with the faculty affiliate, she explained that the LLC had gotten too big for all the students to take the common first-year experience course connected to the LLC, so students were split across two courses, neither of which was designated specifically for the LLC. The faculty affiliate taught one of the courses and a colleague from the sport management department, who was not involved in the LLC, taught the other. The faculty affiliate indicated that she had a closer relationship with the students in her section than she did with LLC students in the other section, even though the course helped to foster those students' connection with each other.

At the advanced level, rigorous academic content is formalized and integrated. It serves to connect students to each other vis-à-vis the course and to foster a deeper connection with faculty affiliated with the LLC. At this level, courses for credit are offered that are specifically designed for the LLC and taken by all LLC students. In addition, to promote integration, there is often a culminating experience for students, which might take the form of a portfolio, capstone or research project. The residential colleges at the University of North Carolina – Greensboro offer an example of the advanced level. Students who live in the residential colleges take some courses together with their specific community, some courses with the broader residential college community composed of students from all the residential colleges, and some courses with the general population of UNCG students. The two-year general curriculum they take while living in the residential college is meant to fulfill their general education requirements. During their final semester in the community, students complete a research-based capstone project that is meant to help them to integrate their learning across the two years.

FACULTY SUPPORT AND ADVOCACY

In addition to rigorous academic content, the intellectual experience of an LLC relies upon faculty support and advocacy. Although the roles of faculty in LLCs vary, faculty support and advocacy typically takes the form of the faculty helping to advance the goals, implementation, and sustainability of the LLC. Ideally, this support should be cultivated from the outset, ensuring that faculty have the opportunity to weigh in on and shape the goals and objectives of the LLC and begin to help foster an academically engaged climate. It becomes most pronounced within the intellectual experience, where faculty play a role in ensuring the LLC inspires the life of the mind in addition to deep social engagement. At the foundational level, faculty should have a specific affiliation with a particular LLC and understand and support the goals of the community. In addition, faculty may help to enact theme-aligned activities that promote intellectual engagement. They may also support recruitment events, discussing the LLC with prospective students, hosting information sessions, or helping with marketing materials. By virtue of their participation in the LLC, these faculty advocates are likely to know and have interacted with peer mentors affiliated with the community.

Interestingly, a single LLC may have several different faculty roles affiliated with their LLCs, which might result in faculty advocates that can satisfy differing levels of the typology. For example, the faculty fellows in Hereford Residential College at the University of Virginia provide a glimpse of what the foundational level might look like. Hereford often taps the fellows affiliated with the LLC to provide theme-based activities that relate to the faculty member's research. One example includes a guided tour conducted by a UVA faculty member and faculty fellow who has done research on the role enslaved labor played in building Thomas Jefferson's original buildings for the University. The tour shows Hereford students, staff, and fellows around the iconic UVA Lawn, but from a perspective previously hidden about the legacy of slavery and Jim Crow.

In contrast, the Principal of Hereford, who is also a faculty member, provides an example of faculty advocacy at the intermediate, perhaps approaching advanced level. The role of the principal is to provide support for the residential college as an intellectual hub, overseeing the implementation of program goals and objectives, living in the residential college, and serving as an advocate of the program at the university level. In addition, the principal is heavily involved with recruitment of students in the LLC. One of the principals we interviewed at the University of North Carolina – Greensboro explained that, in addition to overseeing the academic dimensions of the community, he worked in conjunction with residence life to ensure that peer mentors were contributing to the intellectual experience of the community. He worked to ensure these mentors were organizing study groups and providing support for other academic activities in the residential college, including programming.

STUDENT SUPPORT

Student support is vital to the creation of the intellectual experience of an LLC. This support spans both the intellectual and social experience (thus, it is also addressed in Chapter 6) and can be formal or informal. The seeds of student support for the intellectual experience are planted in the climate of the LLC (Chapter 4), as it is in the ethos of an academically engaging climate that the intellectual experience begins to be cultivated. Peers can provide support for the intellectual experience in a variety of ways, including through formal leadership positions, peer mentoring, or study group facilitation. At the foundational level, student support will likely be a matter of convenience. When resident assistant or other residence hall leadership positions are open, preference will be given to students who have had prior experience in the LLC. California Polytechnic Institute has followed this model, seeking resident assistants who have previous experience in the LLCs so that they can be helpful in sharing their experiences with students. Much of the coordination of study groups and other LLC academic initiatives is conducted by faculty and full-time staff affiliated with the community.

At the intermediate level, student support takes the form of paid peer mentors who have a formal role in fostering the intellectual experience of the LLC. This support might take the form of organizing study groups, conducting peer tutoring, or assisting with academic programming. Rider University's Science LLC offers a clear example of the intermediate level of student support. The Science LLC targets first-year students who are majoring in the sciences. It occupies one residence hall floor that has about 70 beds. There are eight peer mentors on the floor who are hired by the faculty affiliate. These mentors are all science students who provide tutoring and assistance to students on the floor. The floor also has a community advisor (Rider's term for an RA) from residence life. In essence, the peer mentors are charged with supporting students' intellectual development, whereas the community advisors address students' social development.

At the advanced level, student support for the community is even more integrated. Paid peer mentors work in conjunction with faculty advocates to advance the aims of the LLC. This integrated approach might take the form of helping to teach the courses affiliated with the LLC or embedded tutoring, where the peer mentor sits in the class alongside students, meets with the faculty affiliate to understand where students are struggling, and then enacts tutoring sessions that advance the aims of the community. Grogan Residential College at the University of North Carolina – Greensboro provides an example of what advanced peer support would look like. In Grogran, teaching interns, who are paid undergraduate students, help faculty to teach the residential college's courses and conduct their study sessions. These students work in conjunction with the faculty to advance the aims of the courses in which they are embedded.

MAJOR/CAREER ACTIVITIES

The intellectual experience of an LLC is enhanced by major- or career-related activities that help to foster a sense of curiosity and connect students more deeply to the applied aspects of their major or focus of the community. These activities include career workshops, study groups, worksite visits, and other programming that helps students imagine a future that includes the topic or major associated with their LLC. At the foundational level, the LLC encourages students to seek out these resources on campus by attending career workshops or exploring worksites or internships of interest to them. The LLC may also facilitate student use of common space for students to study together. At the University of North Carolina – Greensboro, for example, the career services center on campus has recently begun to target specific residential college cohorts for programming. The programming will include resume development, professional development workshops, and other future-oriented information meant to help students learn more about their interest areas and prepare for life after college.

At the intermediate level, the LLC takes a more active role in ensuring students have opportunities to explore their futures and engage with peers around academic matters. LLC personnel coordinate career activities and/or connect with industry partners and invite them to interact with students in a meaningful way. In addition, as opposed to leaving student study groups to serendipity, LLC personnel coordinate tutoring for LLC courses within the residence hall to encourage students to engage with each other about intellectual matters. The LLCs at Bucknell take advantage of a common hour to advance career- and major-related activities. Senior fellows affiliated with the LLC utilize this time to organize field trips, bring in guest speakers, or take students into the community to engage in service or other activities. In the Rider University Science community, similar activities are provided. The faculty affiliate in the community organizes several field trips throughout the year to facilitate deeper engagement with science, including a trip to the beach to collect biological samples and conduct a beach clean up.

At the advanced level, the connection between the LLC and career discernment is even more tightly bound. The LLC may have industry partners that provide opportunities for real-life experiences related to the LLC theme. These experiences align with students' interests and help with their career discernment. Resources are provided by the LLC to take students on field trips to engage with industry partners or engage in meaningful academic experiences. Organizational structures are in place to help facilitate thoughtful career development. For example, the faculty affiliated with the LLCs at Elon University are required to develop an LLC-specific syllabus (that complements syllabi for LLC courses). This syllabus outlines the learning outcomes associated with the LLC and the activities students will engage in throughout the year. These activities might include field trips to visit sports facilities (sport management and media LLC), engagement with industry professionals (communications LLC), or a for-credit trip to learn more about the industry. Travel might serve as another way to integrate career discernment into an LLC. Prior to the start of the COVID-19 pandemic, Hereford Residential College at the University of Virginia sponsored a spring break trip to Shanghai and Suzhou, China. While there, students conducted research on a topic of their choice. Projects included air pollution in China, modern perspectives on the Shanghai "Marriage Market," and the disappearance of traditional Chinese neighborhoods during economic expansion.

CONCLUSION

When taken as a whole, the intellectual experience layer of the revised BPM emphasizes a deepening of students' curiosity and engagement in the community. It is predicated upon clear goals and objectives, resources, and the establishment of an engaged climate. The intellectual experience is bolstered by deep and meaningful academic content, dedicated faculty who develop relationships with students, engaged peer mentors who play a role in ensuring academic engagement outside of class, and activities that are planned to help students discern and explore their interests and envision pathways to future careers. The typology below (Figure 5.2) offers a way for LLC administrators to initiate conversations about the intellectual experience in the LLC. As readers peruse the typology, some questions to ask include the following:

1. In which dimensions of the academic experience is your LLC strong?
2. Who is involved, and who should be more involved in ensuring a robust academic experience in your LLC?
3. How might you align the intellectual experience with other outcomes of the community?

Attribute	Foundational	Intermediate	Advanced
Theme-aligned Activities and Supports			
Rigorous academic content	Non-credit bearing courses, workshops, or discussion series Guest lectures from university faculty	For credit courses offered by academic department and dovetailed with LLC Service learning opportunities with companion discussion series	For credit courses designed specifically for LLC Culminating experience (e.g., portfolio, capstone, research project)
Faculty support & advocacy	Faculty have specific affiliation with a particular LLC Faculty understand and support the goals of the program Faculty enact theme-aligned activities that promote intellectual engagement Faculty attend recruitment events Faculty know peer mentors and have incidental interaction with them	Faculty are involved in the continued revision of program goals and objectives Faculty work with the residence life staff on theme-aligned activities Faculty are teaching LLC courses Faculty advocate at the departmental level for LLCs Faculty are involved with recruitment of students to the LLC Faculty meet with peer mentors and residence life staff regularly to plan and provide program updates	Faculty are co-leading academic content of the LLC in conjunction with residence life Faculty live in the residence hall/LLC Faculty advocate at the university level for LLCs Faculty and residence life staff work together to integrate curricular and co-curricular aims Faculty create long-term sustainability initiatives and recruitment plans in conjunction with LLC administrator and residence life staff Faculty supervise or co-supervise LLC peer mentors

Figure 5.2 Intellectual Experience Typology.

Major/career activities	Students attend career workshops offered on campus	Students attend career activities coordinated by the LLC	The LLC helps with career discernment specific to the LLC theme and students' interests (e.g. internships, workshops, LLC has a relationship with industry leaders, facilitation of interests, opportunities for application of career interests/career discovery)
	Students use common space to study together	The LLC provides tutoring for LLC courses within the residence hall	
	Students are encouraged to visit worksites of interest and explore internships/co-ops	Industry partners are invited to the LLC to interact with students	
			The LLC has industry partners that provide opportunities for real-life experience related to the LLC theme
			Students initiate and engage in ongoing group study about the LLC theme
			LLC resources are utilized to take students on field trips to industry partners
Student support (Peers/Peer Mentors; Peer Study Group Facilitators)	Prior affiliation with LLC is a consideration in hiring student leaders (RAs, community mentors)	Paid peer mentors have a formal role in fostering the intellectual experience of the community (organize study groups, assist with programming)	Paid peer mentors work in conjunction with faculty advocates to advance the aims of the LLC

Figure 5.2 Continued

REFERENCES

Jessup-Anger, J. E. (2012). Examining how residential colleges inspire the life of the mind. *Review of Higher Education, 35*(3), 431–462.

Jessup-Anger, J. E., Armstrong, M., & Johnson, B. (2020). The role of social justice living-learning communities (LLCs) in promoting students' understanding of social justice and LLC involvement. *Review of Higher Education, 43*(2), 837–860.

Jessup-Anger, J. E., & Benjamin, M. (2023). Engaging students in LLCs. In L. Lomicka & J. Eidum (Eds.), *The faculty factor: Developing faculty engagement with living learning communities* (pp. 164–179). Sterling, VA: Routledge.

Kuh, G. D. (2008). *High-impact educational practices: What they are, who has access to them, and why they matter*. Washington, DC: Association of American Colleges and Universities.

Kuh, G. D., O'Donnell, K., & Reed, S. (2013). *Ensuring quality and taking high-impact practices to scale*. Washington, DC: Association of American Colleges and Universities.

Kuh, G. D., O'Donnell, K., & Schneider, C. G. (2017). HIPs at ten. *Change: The Magazine of Higher Learning, 49*(5), 8–16. doi: 10.1080;00091383.2017.1366805

Wawrzynski, M. R., Jessup-Anger, J. E., Helman, C., Stolz, K., & Beaulieu, J. (2009). Exploring students' perceptions of academically based living-learning communities. *College Student Affairs Journal, 28*, 138–158.

Chapter 6

Best Practices in Living-Learning Communities: Social Experience

Coordinated by faculty, professional staff, peer leaders, and living-learning community (LLC) students themselves, the social element of LLCs aids in building community and sense of belonging within the LLC. Spanierman et al. (2013) found that LLC students, as compared to non-LLC residence hall students, experienced a higher sense of community and belonging, noting the importance of informal peer interactions that are part of the social experience. Because students interact with each other on a daily basis as a result of the residential element, LLCs have the opportunity to regularly support engagement, fitting with Gillen-O'Neel's (2021) conclusions that sense of belonging helps maintain student engagement. Mayhew et al. (2016) highlighted benefits of LLCs, including diversity appreciation and student retention. They stated, "The relatively positive findings for LLCs may be the result of the greater academic and social opportunities that are offered to – and sometimes required of – participating students" (p. 546). Although LLCs may be structured for upper-division students, most focus on first-year students who likely benefit from the way LLCs incorporate them into a community, through the social experience, as they find their place at and establish a connection to the institution.

Underrepresented students are a specific population that may experience gains from LLC social opportunities. First-generation students, in particular, may benefit (Gillen-O'Neel, 2021; Inkelas et al., 2007). Eidum et al. (2020) found that first-generation students may not feel socially connected, and that LLCs can provide a structure for them to interact with both faculty and peers. For first-year students of color on predominantly White campuses, LLCs specifically designed for racial/ethnic minority students can provide a "safe haven and cultural validation" (Han et al., 2018, p. 118). Within the residence hall, Resident Assistant (RA) community efforts are valued generally, and they are particularly vital to the experience of support for students of color (Boettcher et al., 2019). Thus, the LLC staffing structure may be especially beneficial for marginalized students.

DOI: 10.4324/9781003445784-6

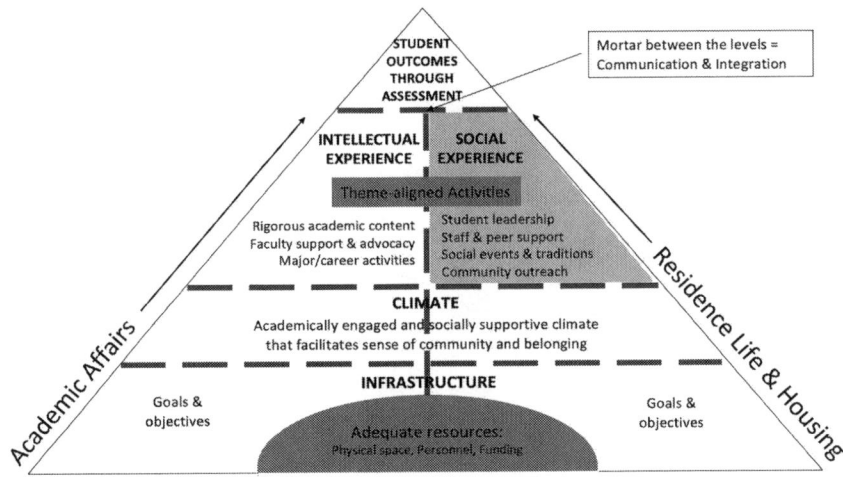

Figure 6.1 The Social Experience of the Revised Best Practices Model.

As indicated in Figure 6.1, Residence Life & Housing may take the lead in coordinating the social experience in hall given their overall responsibilities within the building, but Academic Affairs often contributes to the planning of LLC cocurricular initiatives that promote social integration. Activities may be theme-aligned, such as a recycling collection event for a sustainability-themed LLC or a science fair for girls at a local school coordinated by a women-in-science-themed LLC, and serve to reinforce the focus of the LLC while aiding students in seeing the integration of the intellectual and social experiences of the program. General community-building activities such as LLC retreats and welcoming events are also important social components. Even informal, serendipitous social events such as an ice cream outing, impromptu movie viewings, and the like help create students' sense of membership and community.

The revised Best Practices Model (BPM) (Figure 6.1) highlights four elements of the social experience that are commonly noted as valuable: student leadership, staff and peer support, social events and traditions, and community outreach. Each element is highlighted with examples below and represented in the Social Experience Typology (Figure 6.2).

STUDENT LEADERSHIP

We differentiate student leadership from peer support by defining student leadership as opportunities for the LLC participants to take on "official" roles coordinating activities and providing advisory guidance to the faculty and staff LLC leaders. Peer support, explained in the next section, highlights the formal and informal roles available to upper division students to provide guidance to current LLC participants, often in a mentoring capacity. Student leadership takes a number of forms, from student involvement in program planning to committee membership and hall/LLC governments. Evidence indicates that involvement in student organizations has an overall positive impact on valued student outcomes, such as the development of civic values, retention, and graduation (Mayhew et al., 2016), and involvement in these leadership opportunities gives LLC participants ownership of elements of their learning community experience. Additionally, Dugan (2017) noted that leadership is connected to things we care about and these leadership opportunities may create greater affinity for the organization.

At the foundational level of the Social Experience Typology, LLC students participate in the overall residence hall governance or participate in planning hall programs and events. Although this student leadership involvement is beneficial to the entire residence hall, it may be less connected to the LLC. However, their involvement at this level may lead to greater involvement, as described in the intermediate level of the typology. At this level, LLC students may specifically represent the LLC on hall government and not just assist with programming but initiate programming, perhaps related to the LLC focus or theme. Student leadership at the advanced level includes LLC students taking on formal leadership positions or executive board roles in hall government, initiating programming and working collaboratively with the RA to plan and execute activities. Examples of student leadership at these various levels follow.

Students in Ashby Residential College at the University of North Carolina – Greensboro, along with the Residential College Coordinator, organize the co-curriculum through a hall council structure in Mary Faust Hall where the LLC is housed. Because the residential college comprises the entire building, all students (with rare exceptions) are Residential College participants, and all building activities are RC-focused. Different committees are formed based on student interest, so one year there may be a music appreciation committee or a service committee, but as interests change, new committees are formed and prior ones are discontinued. At a broader level, a student representative from each of the three Residential Colleges at UNCG serves in an official leadership role on the student advisory committee overseen by the university's Director of Residential Colleges.

Due to its tradition of student self-governance, the students in Hereford Residential College at the University of Virginia play a significant role in the running of the College. The Hereford Student Senate (HSS) consists of 30–40 members, with eight executive-level positions. They oversee a substantial budget, garnered from student fees (over $20,000 annually), and use the funds to develop programs, provide resources, and in general improve the Hereford community. It is the HSS that often determines the programs and events for Hereford College, and the staff work to assist them in their planning.

Governance or programming leadership can be a gateway into peer support roles, discussed in the next section. These leadership opportunities, offered to more experienced students, provide benefits to both the students receiving the support and the upper division students who take on the roles. Staff and faculty support are also critical elements for the LLC student experience.

STAFF & PEER SUPPORT

Staff and peers serve as primary supports for the social experience, with faculty and peers being the main supports for the intellectual experience (addressed in Chapter 5). Formal staff support includes RLH professionals, graduate students, and resident assistants/community advisors who are hired by RLH, while selected peer mentors or student volunteers serve as peer support. Additionally, LLC faculty can play a role in the social experience. Faculty, RLH staff, and peer support may structure their work as a team or have separate responsibilities that address the needs of the whole student. Having a support team benefits students, as noted by Felten and Lambert (2020):

> Individual relationships can be educationally powerful, but a network of overlapping relationships is more likely to meet a student's evolving needs than any single mentor can. A web of student-student, student-faculty, and student-staff relationships creates a more resilient resource for a student to draw upon when the going gets tough – and offers institutions a more scalable approach to reaching every student, because faculty and staff can contribute their distinct expertise to support students.
>
> (p. 15)

Creating this support system as a "web" makes clear the interconnected nature of the LLC experience.

Professional RLH support at the foundational level of the typology might include these staff members being generally aware of the goals and objectives of the LLC. They may not be charged with implementing them, but they are aware of the initiatives. At the intermediate level, these staff members actively contribute to LLC goals and initiatives, while at the advanced level, the professional RLH staff members collaborate with LLC leadership to advance the goals and objectives of the program. Although parallel partnerships can be effective (Inkelas et al., 2012), coordinated efforts can help staff and faculty avoid duplicating efforts and conflicting schedules, and allow students to see the integrated nature of the elements of their LLC. Additionally, collaborative programming can lead to positive resource stewardship and consistent messaging to LLC students. At Rider University, for example, the RLH Community

Director, the Community Assistants (CAs), and LLC Coordinator regularly discuss programming and partner to implement it. The CAs are required to do three to four programs a semester and are asked to focus at least half of them on the LLC theme. Recognizing that students have interests outside of the theme, the CAs also focus on programming that will help students integrate socially within and outside the community. The affiliated faculty are always invited to, and typically attend, these events. One example is a kickball game in which the students from the science LLC compete against other students in the hall. Faculty attend the event and talk casually with the students as they play.

Placing a Resident Assistant/Community Advisor on the floor to serve as a leader and support for students is common practice in residence halls. Their responsibilities typically include policy enforcement, facilities management, and programming/community building. Similar typology elements fit for these student RLH staff members, with foundational level behaviors being simple awareness of the programs, intermediate level involving active support and contribution, and advanced level involving greater collaboration. Ideally, RAs/CAs and LLC faculty/staff work collaboratively to coordinate the social experience within the residence hall. Some LLC programs work collaboratively with RLH to select former LLC participants as RAs/CAs on the LLC floor. In other cases, RLH staff place the RA, perhaps with some attention to their academic major so that it reflects the LLC theme. Of course, when RLH staff and LLC faculty/staff work separately, there may be no coordination of the RA placement. Rider University's CAs are hired by the housing professionals, but they consult LLC faculty/staff, and the LLC CAs' job description differs from the general CA description. While this difference initially looked like more work for the CAs, RLH highlighted the benefits of serving as a CA on an LLC floor, such as additional programming funds. For the Sport Management and Media LLC at Elon University, the faculty coordinator was not involved in the hiring of the RLH student staff. However, the faculty coordinator can and has recommended a student from the academic program to be placed on the LLC floor, stating that the most successful year of the program was the year that placement occurred.

While LLC alumni living on the floor may offer informal support by attending LLC activities and interacting with current LLC students, as noted at the foundational level of the typology, structured peer mentor roles are a common element of the peer support structure in many LLCs, reflected in the intermediate and advanced levels. These peer mentor positions may be paid or volunteer positions, although we advocate for paid positions to encourage students to take the role seriously and also to ensure equity for students who need to work while in college. Unlike the RA role, peer mentors typically have little or no responsibility for policy enforcement or facilities issues. They may live within the LLC community, as do the volunteer upper-class mentors in Ashby College at UNCG who receive the benefit of having first choice of rooms in the older residence hall that has an array of room sizes (the mentors have first choice of the larger rooms), or they may live outside of the community but spend time in the LLC in their support roles. Typically, these mentors are former LLC participants who can draw on their own experiences to provide support and guidance to new LLC students. Coordination of community-building activities may be one element of their role. In UNCG's Grogan College, this role is titled Community Ambassador, and these students complete a 1-credit leadership course. They organize core traditions discussed in the next section and also encourage LLC students to initiate programming. As noted in Chapter 5, peer mentors may also have specific responsibilities related to the intellectual experience of the LLC. An example of this academic peer staff support is the Bucknell Residential Colleges Program (RCP) undergraduate "Junior Fellows" role. Junior Fellows play a substantial role in community life, working directly with the faculty teaching in the RCP to help teach the courses and provide the cocurricular activities that align with those courses. They also provide peer mentorship to the students in the LLC and work closely with RAs to build community with their programming.

There are multiple benefits to incorporating peer support roles. While the LLC students benefit from the assistance and guidance, the mentors themselves reap benefits as well. Felten and Lambert (2020) highlighted the benefit of paid mentor positions for the mentors: they develop professional skills and engage more deeply with the institution while earning money. Additionally, the mentors learn more about support available at the institution, which can help the students they mentor as well as the mentors themselves. Finally, peer mentors may better reflect the diversity of the student population, offering opportunities for students to connect with others who share their identities.

Although most LLCs target first-year students, for those programs in which returning students continue as members, these students also serve as support for the social experience, perhaps in informal roles. Current LLC students also can provide assistance for each other as they experience similar challenges. In the informal support capacity at the foundational level of the typology, students identify and are identifiable to others as part of the LLC community, suggesting their "place" of belonging. At the intermediate level of informal support, students recognize the role of the LLC community in providing them with social integration, perhaps looking to the LLC for social opportunities. Finally, at the advanced level, students actively offer support and fellowship to their LLC peers because of their common affiliation.

SOCIAL EVENTS AND TRADITIONS

In *Campus Life: A Search for Community* (1990), the Carnegie Foundation for the Advancement of Teaching asserted the importance of "A Celebrative Community," stating, "... rites, ceremonies, and celebrations unite the campus and give students a sense of belonging to something worthwhile and enduring" (p. 55). They note that these activities should be fun, and that this sense of community must be recreated regularly through these events because of the regular turnover within college and university communities. This kind of celebrative community is important for LLCs as a micro-community within the larger institution. Traditions help the students develop an LLC identity and offer shared experiences that aid in the sustainability of LLCs. Social events are often common traditions, along with welcome/concluding activities for the community and "swag" (i.e., items with the LLC's brand on it) distributed to members. Any number of interruptions can cause traditions to lose their staying power. For example, the recent pandemic disrupted many campus traditions, and while some traditions such as Homecomings and the like may have weathered the disruption, other traditions may have virtually disappeared. Traditions in LLCs may have to be reinvented or reintroduced if such disruptions occur.

Limited traditions are in place and students are encouraged to attend social events at the foundational level of the Social Experience Typology. These events may offer the social activity that students seek, but they lack the spirit of tradition that regularly scheduled events provide. At the intermediate level, students attend university social events as an LLC community and LLC traditions are enacted each year by the LLC leadership. LLC students may attend the club and organization fair as a group each year, perhaps at the recommendation of LLC faculty and staff. Or students may participate in an annual LLC service project coordinated for them by LLC leadership. Students take a lead role in planning social events for the LLC and university community at the advanced level, and LLC students and peer mentors initiate and maintain LLC traditions at this level.

Starting and concluding the academic year with traditions is a regular occurrence in LLCs. The University of Maryland's Gemstone Honors Program hosts a pre-semester overnight retreat, Gems Camp, which increases participants' sense of belonging in the Gemstones Program (Bowers et al., 2020). Hereford Residential College at the University of Virginia hosts their Alpha Convocation and Banquet each year to welcome new members to the community and concludes the year with the Omega Ceremony and Banquet to say goodbye to graduates. Rider University also kicks off the year with a tradition; the Science LLC holds a beginning BBQ that is co-planned by LLC and RLH staff.

Traditional activities and events might include LLC t-shirts, special meals, sporting events, and participation as a community in larger university activities. UVA's Hereford College holds a Tuesday breakfast club and Thursday dessert night. Elon University's Sport Management and Media LLC annually visits the Duke University sport facility, which is very popular with sport management students. Students in the University of North Carolina – Greensboro's Grogan Residential College participate in sports competitions and coordinate events such as Night of the Arts and Masquerade Ball.

Other traditional events occur around holiday themes. At UNCG, Ashby Residential College's Haunted House is an over 25-year-old event that uses a theme connected to a course being taught in the fall. Faustgiving in Ashby is a Thanksgiving dinner named for Mary Faust Hall where the LLC is located and involves both food and exploring the history of the holiday. Hereford Residential College at UVA celebrates Spring Lunar New Year with a banquet. The continuation of these activities each year gives LLC students a unique opportunity to have common experiences from year to year and share a special sense of community as a result.

COMMUNITY OUTREACH

The revised BPM highlights general community outreach opportunities as valuable in the social environment. Whether that outreach involves LLC students going into the community for such activities as tutoring at a local school or inviting the community to the campus for something like an arts festival, interactions beyond the campus are valuable to the social experience.

At the foundational level of the Social Experience Typology, students engage in volunteer opportunities within the university community, perhaps participating in community clean-up events and the like, while at the intermediate level, the LLC has an established partnership with an organization within the community that includes student involvement in service activities related to the organization. Advanced level community outreach may include LLC service-learning courses that include both service activities along with structured learning reflection opportunities.

Each LLC at California Polytechnic Institute – San Luis Obispo has a community partner, and LLC leadership tries to create collaborations that match the LLC theme such as an Engineering LLC partnership with Habitat for Humanity. In some instances, RLH professional staff sit on the boards of the organizations as well, creating an even stronger connection. At UNCG, money raised by the Ashby Haunted House is donated to a local nonprofit organization. Ashby

Residential College also hosts guest speakers from the community. Although it may be appealing to create permanent partnerships for volunteerism, Ashby's director noted that it can be challenging due to limited staffing.

Where the social experience occurs depends on the activity, but appropriate space is necessary. Whether it means having access to playing fields and courts for volleyball or kick-ball tournaments, gathering space for coffee hours, or even transportation to locations outside of campus, LLC leaders must consider what resources are needed and available to them as they coordinate the social experience.

CONCLUSION

A theme-aligned social experience within the revised BPM includes student leadership, staff and peer support, social events and traditions, and community outreach. Developing LLCs may find the foundational level of the typology most reasonable as they establish the various elements of the program. Established LLCs are encouraged to find ways to enhance this aspect of the model through suggestions listed at the intermediate and advanced levels for greater depth of experience for students and further institutionalization and sustainability for the LLC program. As you read through the typology, consider these questions about your LLC:

1. What formal and informal student leadership opportunities already exist? Which could be added or deleted? How can you encourage LLC students to step into these formal and informal leadership roles?
2. How do RLH staff and other LLC personnel work together? What are the challenges and what successes have you had?
3. How are social activities coordinated? How are staff trained for this aspect of their role?
4. What traditions exist? What traditions would you like to start or eliminate?
5. What opportunities for community outreach exist? What community outreach is already established at the institution such that the LLC could collaborate?

Attribute	Foundational	Intermediate	Advanced
Theme-aligned Activities and Supports			
Student leadership opportunities	LLC students participate in hall governance LLC students assist in planning programs and events	LLC students serve as leaders in hall governance and have designated LLC roles (LLC representative to hall council if entire building is not LLC) LLC students initiate programming	LLC students serve on LLC governance as participants and leaders LLC students co-program with Resident Assistant staff
Staff & peer support (formal/informal)	**Formal**		
	Professional RLH staff are aware of the goals and objectives of the LLC Resident Assistant is aware of the goals and objectives of the LLC LLC alumni attend LLC activities and interact with current LLC students	Professional RLH staff actively contribute to LLC initiatives Resident Assistant actively contributes to LLC initiatives Designated LLC peer mentors provide support to current LLC students	Professional RLH staff collaborate with LLC leadership to advance LLC goals and objectives Resident Assistant collaborates with LLC leadership to advance LLC goals and objectives LLC peer mentors live on the residence hall floor, and collaborate with LLC leadership to provide programmatic initiatives
	Informal		
	Students identify and are identifiable to others as part of an LLC community	Students recognize the role of the community in providing them with social integration	Students actively offer support/fellowship to peers because of their common affiliation

Figure 6.2 Social Experience Typology.

BEST PRACTICES IN LIVING-LEARNING COMMUNITIES: SOCIAL EXPERIENCE

Social events and traditions	Students are encouraged to attend LLC social events Limited traditions are enacted annually	Students attend university-sponsored social events as an LLC community LLC traditions are enacted annually and maintained primarily by LLC leadership	Students are planning and leading social events for the LLC and/or university community LLC traditions are initiated, maintained, and anticipated by students and/or peer mentors
Community outreach	LLC students engage in volunteer opportunities within the university community	The LLC has established partnerships with the community and engages students in service within the community	LLC courses offer service learning experiences for LLC students and reflect on these experiences in light of LLC goals

Figure 6.2 Continued

REFERENCES

Boettcher, M. L., Eason, A., Earnest, K., & Lewis, L. (2019). The cultivation of support networks by students of color in a residence hall setting at a predominantly white institution. *Journal of College and University Student Housing, 45*(2), 30–46.

Bowers, M. E., Tobin, L. K., Lee, J., Skendall, K. C., & Coale, F. J. (2020). Increasing campus sense of belonging through LLC participation: To Gems Camp we go. *Learning Communities Research and Practice, 8*(1), Article 2. Retrieved from https://washingtoncenter.evergreen.edu/lcrpjournal/vol8/iss1/2

Carnegie Foundation for the Advancement of Teaching. (1990). *Campus life: In search of community*. Princeton, NJ: Princeton University Press.

Dugan, J. P. (2017). *Leadership theory: Cultivating critical perspectives*. San Francisco, CA: Jossey-Bass.

Eidum, J., Lomicka, L., Chiang, W., Endick, G., & Stratton, J. (2020). Thriving in residential learning communities. *Learning Communities Research and Practice, 8*(1), Article 7. Retrieved from https://washingtoncenter.evergreen.edu/lcrpjournal/vol8/iss1/7

Felten, P., & Lambert, L. M. (2020). *Relationship-rich education: How human connections drive success in college*. Baltimore, MD: Johns Hopkins University Press.

Gillen-O'Neel, C. (2021). Sense of belonging and student engagement: A daily study of first- and continuing-generation college students. *Research in Higher Education, 62*, 45–71.

Han, S., Dean, M., & Okoroji, C. (2018). Minority student experiences in a living and learning community on a predominately white college campus. *Journal of Ethnographic & Qualitative Research, 13*, 107–121.

Inkelas, K., Daver, Z., Vogt, K., & Leonard, J. (2007). Living-learning programs and first-generation college students' academic and social transition to college. *Research in Higher Education, 48*(4), 403–434.

Inkelas, K., Garvey, J., & Robbins, C. (2012, April 16). Best practices in living-learning programming: Results from a multiple case study, presented at Annual Meeting of the American Educational Research Association, Vancouver, British Columbia, 2012.

Mayhew, M. J., Rockenbach, A. N., Bowman, N. A., & Wolniak, G. C. (2016). *How college affects students: 21st century evidence that higher education works* (Vol. 3). San Francisco, CA: Jossey-Bass.

Spanierman, L. B., Soble, J. R., Mayfield, J. B., Neville, H. A., Aber, M., Khuri, L., & De La Rosa, B. (2013). Living learning communities and students' sense of community and belonging. *Journal of Student Affairs Research and Practice, 50*(3), 308–325.

Chapter 7

Best Practices in Living-Learning Communities: Student Outcomes Through Assessment

As readers of our 2018 book will recall, the Living-Learning Communities (LLC) Best Practices Model was based on a series of building blocks arranged in a four-level pyramid. We also asserted that an effective LLC assessment plan examined (a) the extent to which the LLC's various building blocks are aligned with the program's goals and objectives; (b) the effectiveness of the discrete building blocks of the program in achieving those goals and objectives; and (c) the level of integration of the various building blocks to form a unified program. We described the extent to which assessments guided the design and delivery of an LLC as "the mortar between the bricks," or the figurative glue that held the blocks of the pyramid together to form a cohesive whole.

The decision to include assessment as part of the Best Practices Model received accolades from practitioners who used the model for their work in LLCs, noting that its presence served as a constant reminder that LLCs must continually engage in a cycle of questioning, assessment, and change. Others used the building blocks from the Best Practices Model itself to operationalize the components of their LLCs to be assessed. Still others, while acknowledging the importance of assessment in their work, wondered if there were other facets of the LLC structure that could also serve as mortars holding the bricks of the model together. Some made a compelling case that "communication" could also serve as the model's "glue," while we also felt that "integration" played a similar role. Indeed, we felt that integration was such a significant piece of the model that we made it the pinnacle of the Best Practices Model pyramid in our 2018 book, signifying that optimal LLCs were not only effective in all other blocks of the model that fell below it but also intentional about integrating the work of the various blocks into a linked entity.

In actuality, assessment, communication, and integration, which are facilitated by both Academic Affairs and Residence Life & Housing, all play interconnected roles in our LLC Best Practices Model. All three constructs are less so discrete blocks on a pyramid, and more like checks and balances that ensure that an LLC is running effectively. Communication warrants that all of the various stakeholders in the LLC are aware of what others are doing. Integration makes it possible to build on different aspects of the LLC that are helping students make connections and apply their knowledge, skills, and abilities in new ways. Ultimately, assessment is the vehicle through which LLCs examine and measure whether they are performing effectively; it also points stakeholders to directions where they can afford to make improvements.

Yet, one of the questions we often fielded from practitioners was how to assess student learning outcomes resulting from LLC participation. The 2018 Best Practices Model offered a template for the operationalization of the various structural components of LLCs, which helped practitioners to identify what aspects of their communities they could assess. Yet, while this strategy illuminated the important organizational portions of LLCs to consider in an assessment plan, it offered no guidance on how to use the Best Practices Model to examine if and how LLCs influence students' academic and social outcomes.

After conversations with LLC practitioners, we have concluded that, for LLC assessments to be effective in reviewing the progress of the community overall, all other levels of the pyramid must be in place. After all, the key components of an LLC to be assessed are facilitated by both Academic Affairs and RLH, with clear goals and objectives as well as resources being essential for programmatic development. It would make no sense, for example, to assess an LLC's resources before creating and implementing the intellectual and social experiences to understand the use of, and need for, various resources. Additionally, LLCs can exist without assessment, but they likely won't last long if data demonstrating their effectiveness is not collected and utilized. Thus, in the revised Best Practices Model (see Figure 7.1), assessment remains a key portion of the model and is thought to rest atop the other layers of the pyramid, or the pinnacle.

However, assessment in and of itself does not constitute the totality of the pinnacle of the pyramid. To address the shortcoming that practitioners identified regarding the lack of specificity on how and where student outcomes fit into the Best Practices Model, we have chosen to title the pinnacle "Assessment through Student Outcomes." Accordingly, LLC assessment is not merely the evaluation of its programs, practices, and activities, but also _how_ those programs, practices, and activities affect the students who engage with them. Meanwhile, communication and integration now form the twin foci of the mortar between the bricks, which will be discussed in greater detail in Chapter 8.

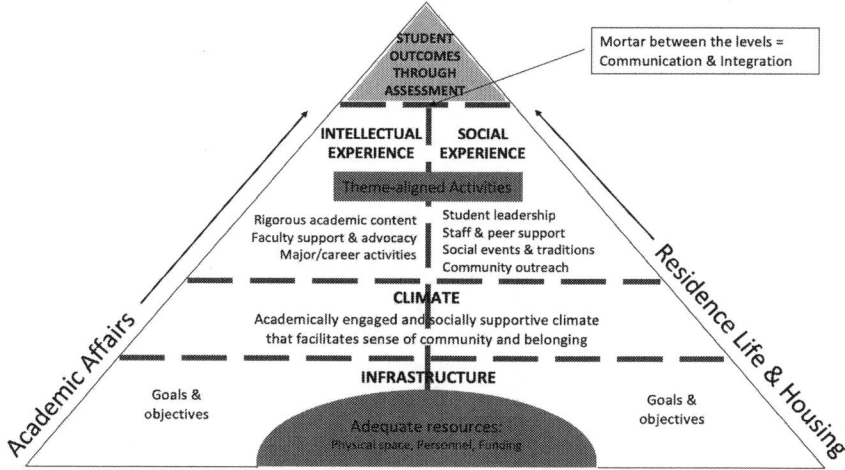

Figure 7.1 Student Outcomes/Assessment in the Revised Best Practices Model.

FORMATIVE AND SUMMATIVE LLC ASSESSMENTS

As a matter of good practice, LLCs should be assessing both their structural components and their impact on students. In fact, one might conceive of the two types of assessment as two parts of a comprehensive package that examines both the formative and summative aspects of LLCs. Formative assessment aims to provide direct feedback to LLC staff during the community's operation. It is more diagnostic in nature and meant to be used to assess the effectiveness of elements of the community and to make changes during the delivery of the program, when possible. Summative assessment, on the other hand, focuses on results, and is typically measured at the end of a process. Summative assessments are more evaluative in nature and meant to assess the overall effectiveness of the community as a whole (Erkens, 2019). For LLCs, this is often reflected as the empirical investigation into how communities bear an influence on their participants' outcomes. Sometimes, summative assessments may be used to determine whether an LLC should be continued or not.

The revised Best Practices Model can be used not only to identify facets of LLCs that facilitate their effectiveness but also to articulate how practices within LLCs can be assessed formatively. It is important for LLC practitioners to know if the different facets of their work are effective, and if the elements of the LLC reflect the goals and objectives for which they serve. For example, the following are important formative assessment questions for LLC practitioners to ask about their program's effectiveness, based on the revised Best Practices Model:

- Are the goals and objectives of the LLC understood and well articulated?
- Are adequate resources in place for achieving those goals and objectives?
- Is the LLC climate supporting students' academic and social success as well as sense of belonging?
- Are the intellectual experiences in the community aligned with and helping to achieve student success with the LLC's goal and objectives?
- Are the social experiences in the community aligned with and helping to achieve student success with the LLC's goal and objectives?
- Is communication effective in this LLC?
- Are the various facets of the LLC, as exemplified in the revised Best Practices Model, integrated with one another?

LLC practitioners who spoke with us about the original Best Practices Model admitted that comprehensive assessments of their LLCs every year were a challenge, especially with limited staff and faculty time that is already stretched thin. However, it is important to emphasize that it is not necessary to assess all elements of one's LLC every year. In fact, that is probably not advisable when considering time and other resource constraints. Instead, LLC practitioners might consider formatively assessing something different each year, such as one level of the pyramid at a time. This would allow for ongoing improvements while not overwhelming the LLC practitioner or the students and other staff. LLC practitioners should consider what information is necessary to collect annually, such as the use of resources or costs per student, but may find that other elements, such as social events and traditions, may not require annual assessment. We do recommend that LLC practitioners take advantage of accessible opportunities to collect feedback, such as quick assessments of theme-aligned activities at the end of events when it is convenient to gather useful information.

In addition to ongoing formative assessments, LLCs should get into the habit of periodically conducting summative assessments. Again, summative assessments are evaluative in nature and are used to examine the overall effectiveness of the LLC as a whole. Such assessments are critical when advocating for the future of the LLC, whether it be requesting additional funding, arguments for its value, or simply justifying its existence. Typically, it would be important to show that the LLC is meeting the goals and objectives that it set for its student participants. Thus, a summative assessment would measure participants' outcomes on the LLC's stated goals/objectives, and likely compare their outcomes to other students at the institution similar in profile but not participating in the LLC. For example, say a particular LLC's objective is to help students find their academic interests and choose a major. That LLC's summative assessment might compare the major adoption rates of its participants with a pool of non-LLC participants at the same university who are demographically and academically similar. In addition to the outcomes aligned with the LLC's goals and objectives, other popular outcomes that are generally of interest to campus leaders include an LLC's overall influence on students' academic achievement (i.e., course grades and grade point averages), retention (e.g., returning after the first year, graduation), and satisfaction with the LLC, university, and their own experiences. LLC practitioners might prioritize their student outcomes of interest for future assessments; in a subsequent portion of this chapter, we will present a logic model that distinguishes student outcomes into short-term, medium-term, and long-term outcomes.

Another group that could potentially be studied summatively are the faculty who take part in the LLCs. In addition to paying attention to the outcomes of student participants in an LLC, the community might consider how faculty are affected by their participation in an LLC. For example, are faculty who engage with LLCs more satisfied with their work at the university than faculty who do not? Do faculty who work with LLCs feel more fulfilled with their vocations? Do they feel more energized and creative about the other aspects of their jobs, such as teaching, scholarship, and service? Do they feel a stronger affiliation with the university? LLCs may be beneficial to not only students, and it would behoove LLCs to ascertain how they benefit the faculty who engage with them.

CONDUCTING LLC ASSESSMENTS

As we noted in the 2018 book, once LLC practitioners have identified what about their communities they wish to study (whether it be a formative or summative question), they can consult with Upcraft and Schuh (1996) in designing their assessment studies:

- Determine whom to study
- Determine how data will be collected
- Determine what instruments will be used
- Determine who should collect the data
- Determine how the data will be analyzed
- Determine the implications of the study for practice
- Report the results and make necessary changes
- Observe the reaction to the changes
- Repeat the process by asking new questions.

Much of the above will be summarized in more detail by using the Assessment typology. However, one of the more common questions we have been asked about assessment concerns whether the LLC should undertake a quantitative or qualitative approach to their assessment. In principle, the answer to that question depends on what is being studied and the questions being asked. For example, it might be difficult to examine the climate of an LLC quantitatively. Instead qualitative interviews, focus groups, or observations might be more desirable for studying a climate. Meanwhile, assessing student participation in the LLC's programs and events is likely best examined through quantitative procedures since the data collection process is largely based on attendance rates. That being said, another aspect to consider is: who is the audience for the assessment? Is it a formative assessment that will be only used to improve functions and processes? Or, is it a summative assessment that will justify the program's current staffing and funding to its School or College leadership? Does the ultimate audience have a strong preference for one approach over the other? For example, does the Dean of the School or College that results for the summative assessment are being prepared for tend to be better convinced using quantitative or qualitative data, or both? A rigorous yet also expedient assessment should take both matters (the nature of the study and the ultimate audience for the assessment) into account when choosing a methodology.

THE ASSESSMENT TYPOLOGY

The typology below (Figure 7.2) offers insights into how to grow and develop more comprehensive and sophisticated LLC assessment designs over time. Users of the revised Best Practices Model can use the typologies associated with each level of the pyramid in the model to assess whether their efforts on that level are foundational, intermediate, or advanced. What's more, LLCs seeking to move up a level from foundational to intermediate or intermediate to advanced can see what constitutes the more advanced level through the typology and make changes to their communities that will enable them to move levels.

For example, when assessing their LLC's climate for academic engagement, practitioners can consult the climate typology. In terms of student participation in programs and events, they can categorize their own levels of student participation in terms of whether: (a) only some – and typically the same set of – students are participating in programming (foundational); (b) most students are participating in programming on a regular basis (intermediate); or (c) nearly all students are participating in programs and events, and students encourage one another to engage (advanced). Accordingly, if the LLC is currently experiencing widespread student participation in programming, but there are currently no ways in which older peers are encouraging newer ones in the community to engage with the LLC's programming, practitioners in that program can brainstorm what existing mechanisms they can utilize to create those conditions. This might be something like creating peer mentor roles in the LLC, or having RAs periodically gather newer students on their floors and accompany them to a community program.

In addition to the typologies we provided for the other levels of the Best Practices Model pyramid, we offer a typology for LLCs' assessment efforts, including graduated levels of practice regarding assessment types, scope, data analysis, reporting, and planning.

Attribute	Foundational	Intermediate	Advanced
Assessment Type (Schuh & Upcraft)	Tracking usage Satisfaction Needs	Attainment of goals/objectives Academic achievement Retention/Persistence Graduation	Learning Outcomes Benchmarking and Professional standards
Assessment Scope	Feedback is collected at individual LLC events	LLC experience is assessed as part of a larger RLH assessment of residential living Individual elements/levels of individual LLCs are assessed	LLCs are an integrated part of comprehensive, campus-wide assessments LLC data integrated with other university data sources
Data Analysis (quantitative)	Descriptive (percentages, means) analysis	Longitudinal analysis to study LLC's relationship to retention, persistence, & graduation	Sophisticated analysis that may require outside assistance (e.g., Institutional Research Office)
Assessment Reporting	Findings are shared with the staff and students of the LLC	Findings are shared more broadly with student affairs and academic affairs divisions directly associated with the LLC	Findings are shared with decision-makers, such as the President and Provost, as well as in recruitment efforts or marketing materials from the institution. IR dashboard just for LLCs (UMD) Findings are shared at professional conferences and in professional publications
Assessment Planning	Assessment of an individual element of the LLC is planned	Assessment of LLC elements is conducted annually on a cycle (e.g., for the Social Level, Student Leadership is assessed one year, Student and Peer Support the next, etc.)	Various elements of the LLC are assessed annually with the assistance of a centralized assessment office or assistance from a centralized learning communities office

Figure 7.2 Assessment Typology.

Types of Assessments

Beginning with the types of assessments LLC could undertake, we borrow from Upcraft and Schuh's (1996) seven approaches to assessment. Like Upcraft and Schuh, we begin at the foundational level with tracking student usage of the LLC's programs, activities, events, and other resources. With today's technology, tracking usage does not need to involve manually taking attendance at gatherings. Instead, LLCs could use ID card swipe data, if their universities require swipes to enter LLC facilities. Or, LLC students could use their phones and a QR code that would lead them to an attendance tracking app. Knowing what proportion of students as well as possibly what kinds of students (gender, major, class year, etc.) attended or used certain functions can help LLCs discern important information such as which programs consistently suffered from attendance problems and which constituencies are not attending targeted programming.

A second foundational type of assessment would include satisfaction assessments. Satisfaction polls should be taken immediately after LLC programming and can gauge how well LLC participants liked or disliked various aspects of the program. These polls can be administered on paper and administered immediately at the end of the program, or students can be provided a hyperlink or QR code to access a survey sometime after the event has ended. While satisfaction assessments can help LLCs identify strengths and weaknesses of their programs, activities, events, and resources, it is important for LLC staff to remember that students' satisfaction with programming should be measured in relationship to how well the offering fulfilled its goals and objectives.

A final foundational assessment type is the needs assessment. This assessment investigates aspects of an LLC that are currently not in existence that students identify as needing, or that LLC faculty and staff determine that students need. Needs assessments can be challenging, especially in terms of distinguishing between students' needs and wants. In order to prioritize which needs should be attended to first, LLCs can consider how well the need is aligned with the LLC's goals and objectives, if the need is feasible and fundable, how much the other stakeholders in the LLC think it is worthwhile to pursue, and if the need appears to be empirically supported in the higher education literature as being a good practice. These three assessment types (tracking usage, satisfaction, and needs) form the most basic of assessment designs for any LLC but are by no means a comprehensive assessment portfolio. In fact, as we move into more advanced forms of assessments in the typology, the assumption is that LLCs will continue to conduct usage, satisfaction, and needs assessments, and in addition, will add new assessment types.

At the intermediate level, if they have not already begun this process, LLCs should be working in earnest to assess whether they are meeting their stated goals and objectives. It is important to underscore that attainment of an LLC's goals and objectives is not the same as individuals' satisfaction with their experiences in the LLC. Just as students' course evaluations are not the equivalent of what they learned in the course, students' satisfaction with their LLC is not the same thing as the fulfillment of the community's goals and objectives. Instead, LLCs will need to find other ways to observe or measure goal/objective attainment, which may involve new forms of data collection that are unfamiliar to practitioners, such as experimental or quasi-experimental designs, longitudinal designs, and more vigorous forms of observations. Consequently, it may be helpful for LLC practitioners to consult with social science methodologists in their institution's School of Education or the Psychology Department for assistance. Yet, there can be no more important assessment question for an LLC than whether or not they are reaching their goals.

Other assessments that go beyond the foundational level are outcomes assessments such as the impact of LLC participation on students' academic achievement, retention/persistence, and graduation rates. These assessments, no doubt, will be of interest to institutional leaders at colleges and universities of all types. Assessing LLC effectiveness in facilitating stronger outcomes like grades, retention, and graduation will require a partnership with the unit at the institution that manages student records. At some institutions, this may be the institutional research office, while at others, it may be the registrar's office. In addition, any examination that purports to analyze whether LLC participation had an impact on the above outcomes must compare LLC students' outcomes with those of a comparable sample of students at the institution who did not participate in that LLC. Finally, a robust outcomes assessment should also measure and control for other aspects of LLC students' college experiences that could also have an impact on their grades, retention, and graduation. Again, this may mean that the LLC practitioners will need to consult with and/or hire individuals with this level of statistical expertise and, perhaps, access to the data. The logic model presented in the next section will illustrate how LLCs can conceptualize these foundational, intermediate, and advanced components in one, comprehensive assessment plan.

At the most advanced level, LLCs can address other learning outcomes that are not directly related to their goals and objectives. For example, if the objectives of the LLC are related to supporting achievement in STEM majors, the LLC may wish to see if participation in their program is related to other goals and objectives identified by their institution, such as appreciation of diverse perspectives. The other type of assessments that could be undertaken at the advanced level are benchmarking and professional standards assessments. Benchmarking evaluations compare aspects of an LLC's functions with other like LLCs, either on the same campus or a different one. Typically, benchmarking assessments are not comprehensive, but instead focus on one or a few facets of an LLC. For example, the Honors LLC at one institution might benchmark with an Honors LLC at another institution on how they recruit faculty engagement and build their course curricula.

Although some LLCs may choose to conduct a benchmarking assessment first before undertaking any other form of assessment, this is not advisable. Benchmarking assessments are best suited for LLCs that already know their strengths and limitations as a result of prior usage, satisfaction, needs, goals and objectives, and other outcomes assessments. This way, when they are benchmarking with another entity, they can better understand how similarities and differences with the benchmarked program may affect their own program's functioning and students' experiences.

Meanwhile, professional standards assessments compare an LLC's effectiveness through references to national or professional standards. In other words, how do an LLC's programs, services, and facilities compare to accepted national standards or professional norms? Currently, the largest clearinghouse of professional standards in student affairs, the Council for the Advancement of Standards (CAS), does not have a set of standards for LLCs, but they do offer standards for the functional area of Residence Life & Housing (RLH). For example, CAS notes that, compared to traditional residence hall students, LLC participants should report a strong sense of institutional belonging and higher levels of academic self-confidence, which can be measured through LLC assessment. In addition to RLH programs, CAS offers standards for student affairs functional areas that may intersect with the themes, goals, and/or objectives of LLCs, including academic advising programs; campus religious, secular, and spiritual programs; career services; civic engagement and service-learning programs; college honor society programs; collegiate recreation programs; disability resources and services; health promotion services; international student programs and services; leadership education and development programs; LGBTQ+ programs; multicultural student programs and services; student media programs; sustainability programs; transfer student programs and services; trio and college access programs; undergraduate research programs; veterans and military-connected programs and services; and women's and gender programs and services.

Scope of Assessments

When LLCs are first beginning their assessment plans, it is likely that the scope of their data collection is limited to feedback from individual LLC programs, events, and resources. Yet, as their assessment portfolios grow, so too do the ways in which LLC assessments are embedded within broader data collections. For example, at the intermediate level, while feedback is still being collected at the LLC level, it could be that LLC students' experiences become a part of broader assessment efforts undertaken at the Residence Life & Housing level.

For example, as RLH offices collect data on student satisfaction and needs in all of their buildings, they can also collect data on behalf of the LLCs. Finally, at the most advanced level, LLC data could similarly be integrated as part of a comprehensive, campus-wide assessment, such as data collected on behalf of the National Survey of Student Engagement (NSSE) or data consolidated for an upcoming accreditation review. Ultimately, LLC data could be integrated with other university data sources collected by a pan-university office, such as the Office of Institutional Research.

Data Analysis (Quantitative)

Quantitative analyses are often sought by institutional leaders to illustrate effectiveness of LLCs. Foundational quantitative analyses are what one might typically find in an administrative report, including descriptive statistics (counts, percentages, means). In order to study the impact of LLC participation on student outcomes (academic achievement, retention, learning outcomes), vigorous assessments will require longitudinal data collections and longitudinal data analytical techniques, such as experimental design analyses and structural equation models. Finally, advanced assessment designs will require even more sophisticated analyses that will likely compel LLC stakeholders to obtain outside assistance from individuals with advanced statistical skills.

Assessment Reporting

As an LLC's assessment portfolio expands, so should its reporting mechanisms. Assessments at the foundational level will likely yield results that should be shared only with the internal stakeholders of the LLC, especially formative data. Meanwhile, as LLCs progress into outcomes assessments, their findings should be more broadly shared with Student and Academic Affairs leadership at their institutions, particularly those whose work intersects with the LLC. Findings from the more advanced types of assessments can move into even broader dissemination, including institutional leaders (president, provost), and into marketing or recruiting materials that reach prospective students, parents, and alumni. Moreover, advanced level assessments would represent some of the most cutting-edge work in LLCs and could and should be shared at professional conferences and in professional publications.

Assessment Planning

Cumulatively, an LLC's assessment plans should continue to grow as the program progresses into more and more advanced levels. At the foundational level, LLCs might "start small" and choose to assess one element of their programming. As they evolve into more intermediate levels of assessment planning, LLCs may begin using an "assessment cycle," during which different aspects of the LLC are assessed annually, one after another. For example, at the Social Experience level of the revised Best Practices Model, an LLC may examine its student leadership programming one year, the staff and peer support the following year, the social events and traditions during the third year, and community outreach efforts in the fourth year. Then, the cycle would start over and re-evaluate the leadership programming in year five. At the most advanced level, the LLC would operate on an assessment cycle, and would be assisted by a centralized assessment office or a centralized learning community office, which would integrate the LLC's work with the university's findings.

PUTTING IT ALL TOGETHER: A COMPREHENSIVE LLC ASSESSMENT MODEL

In reflecting on how we could address both formative and summative aspects of LLC assessment plans, including the examination of student outcomes resulting from LLC participation, we turned to an increasingly popular framework used in higher education as well as the private and public sector: logic models. Indeed, in her Occasional Paper on the comprehensive assessment of high-impact practices, Ashley Finley (2019) recommended the logic model as a tool for evaluating both the implementation of high-impact practices and student outcomes associated with such practices. The term "logic model" is typically credited to Wholey (1979) in *Evaluation: Promise and Performance*. While the term has gone through multiple iterations and variations, logic models are generally described as visual representations developed to operationalize a program's planning, implementation, and evaluation in a way that links investments to outcomes. In their simplest form, logic models include (a) "inputs," or resources that go into a program; (b) "outputs," or activities that the program undertakes; and (c) "outcomes" or "impact," the changes or benefits that result from the utilization of the program's inputs to create and execute the outputs.

Subsequent logic models ("Enhancing Program Performance," 2023) further subdivide the outputs section of a logic model into "activities," or what programs do with their inputs to achieve their objectives, and "participants," or the people reached by the program's activities. In addition, outcomes are typically categorized into three types: (a) "short-term outcomes," or changes directly connected to the program's outputs; (b) "medium-term outcomes," or those that bridge or may result from the establishment of short-term outcomes while also laying the groundwork for the longer-term outcomes; and (c) "long-term outcomes" are ultimate impacts that evolve over time that are generally linked to the program's short- and medium-term outcomes. Before the introduction of the LLC logic model, it is important to distinguish between "outputs" and "outcomes" in logic models: outputs are things that programs do, and outcomes are the ways in which people are affected by the outputs.

The various components of the revised LLC Best Practices Model can be subsumed into a logic model to produce a comprehensive assessment plan for LLCs (see Figure 7.2). The inputs, or LLC resources, of the LLC logic model are borrowed directly from the infrastructure level of the revised Best Practices Model: physical, personnel, and funding resources, as well as goals and objectives derived from both the academic unit and Residence Life & Housing. The outputs, or the activities the LLC undertakes, are the theme-aligned intellectual and social programming created by the community: rigorous academic content, faculty support and advocacy, major/career activities, student leadership, staff and peer support, social events and traditions, and community outreach. The participants interacting with those outputs are the major stakeholders of LLCs: students, faculty, LLC staff, Residence Life & Housing staff, and institutional champions.

Finally, as shown in Figure 7.2, the outcomes are depicted in short-, medium-, and long-term categories. It is critical to emphasize that outcomes associated with LLC participation should be idiosyncratic with the goals and objectives of the particular LLC. For example, outcomes related to participation in a French House will likely relate to enhancements in students concerning French language acquisition and appreciation of French culture. On the other hand, student outcomes for a Wellness LLC might align more with overall well-being, positive outlook, increased empathy, etc. That being said, we offer some short-, medium-, and long-term outcomes in Figure 7.2 as examples. Short-term outcomes, or outcomes directly associated with LLC participation, might include aspects such as greater faculty-student interaction, more peer-to-peer interaction, the creation of a supportive climate, and community connection. LLC medium-term outcomes, or those that bridge the short- and long-term outcomes, could include sense of belonging, interpersonal growth, intellectual stimulation, leadership skills, and civic engagement. Long-term outcomes, or the ones that evolve over time – and perhaps even beyond students' participation in their LLC – might consist of retention or graduation, mature interpersonal relationships, and deepened love of lifelong learning, among others.

Using the above logic model in Figure 7.3, LLC practitioners might conceive of the inputs and outputs of the framework as the portions that should be assessed formatively. For example:

- Are the physical space, personnel, and funding in the LLC adequate for the community's needs?
- How well are the following aspects of the LLC's programming and activities performing?
  - Academic content
  - Faculty involvement
  - Major/career activities
  - Student leadership roles

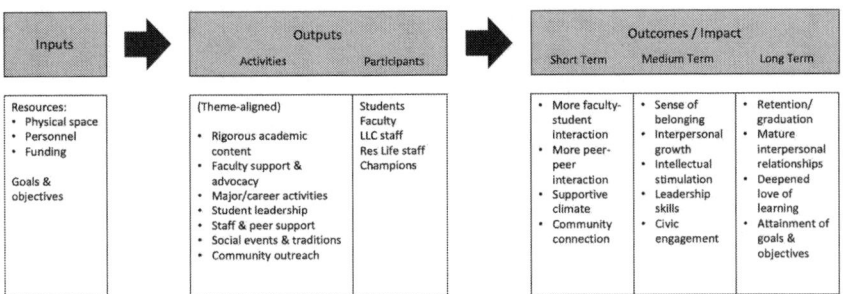

Figure 7.3 A Living-Learning Communities Logic Model.

- Staff and peer support roles
- Social events and traditions
- Community outreach opportunities
- How are the participants or primary LLC stakeholders engaging with the previous programs and activities?

Asking these types of formative assessment questions will help the LLC to identify its strengths and areas for improvement and contribute toward continuous quality improvements. Moreover, to reiterate, LLCs can use the typologies introduced in this book to evaluate if their programs and activities are at the foundational, intermediate, or advanced level, and what they might need to do in order to move up a level.

Then, LLC practitioners can connect their inputs and outputs in their logic models to student outcomes by conducting summative assessments. In other words, they can study whether their LLCs are facilitating positive changes in their student participants. To start, LLCs should track faculty-student and student-student interactions in their communities. They should also conduct assessments of the community's academic and social climate. Beyond these immediate outcomes, LLCs can also create an assessment plan that examines medium- and long-term impacts, such as sense of belonging, interpersonal growth, intellectual stimulation, retention, and deepened love of lifelong learning.

However, it is crucial to underscore that such medium- and long-term outcome assessments will require three methodological considerations: longitudinal data collection, comparison groups, and multivariate analyses. Outcomes that evolve over time, such as medium- and long-term outcomes in logic models, mandate that data be collected during multiple time points, or longitudinally. For example, in order to understand whether a student has an improved maturity in their interpersonal relationships, one must have assessed their level of interpersonal relationship maturity at some earlier point in time (e.g., at the beginning of their participation in the LLC) and then compared it to their level of maturity at a later point in time (e.g., at the end of their LLC participation, or even a year after their participation ended). Furthermore, in order to show that the differences in student outcomes are due to LLC participation, the summative assessment will need to include a comparison group of students who did not participate in the LLC but are similar in background, ability, and motivation. Then, the outcomes for the LLC participants should be compared to those of the non-LLC students. Finally, if the LLC is interested in knowing which aspects or components of its community are contributing to stronger student outcomes, it will need to conduct multivariate analyses that operationalize and measure the community's inputs and outputs that will serve as independent variables in a multivariate analysis to the measured student outcomes that will comprise the dependent variables. This type of analysis demands advanced statistical training, and if the LLC staff does not have someone with these skills, it may need to find and compensate someone at their institution with the requisite skills.

Together, the revised Best Practices Model, the assessment typology, and the logic model combine to provide a comprehensive and rigorous assessment plan for any LLC. Although this combination depicts the "ultimate" assessment framework, it is difficult to achieve in a real-world context. LLC practitioners can think of this combined assessment model as something to strive toward a portion at a time, but not necessarily implement all at once. Indeed, as the next section describes, even the LLCs with well-developed assessment plans have not reached this "pinnacle" in their own work.

EXAMPLES OF LLC ASSESSMENTS

Of all of the blocks on the revised Best Practices Model, it may perhaps be the most difficult to provide examples from LLC practice for the Assessment block. Most LLC practitioners would readily admit that their assessment plans are not as fully developed as the other aspects of their communities. However, because assessment is an area that practitioners find challenging, we wanted to be sure to provide several examples from the current landscape of LLC practice. Instead of interspersing the examples throughout the chapter, though, we are offering a set of examples as short vignettes below.

The Gemstone Program at the University of Maryland, College Park

Gemstone annually conducts foundational assessments of students' experiences with and opinions of their faculty mentors, research team, diversity opportunities, and the program in general. At the intermediate level, because one of their primary objectives is to develop students' leadership abilities, they have partnered with a national study of college student leadership, the Multi-Institutional

Study of Leadership (MSL), to assess Gemstone students' leadership development and compare their outcomes with a national sample. At the advanced level, the Gemstone Program is fortunate to have an institutional assessment infrastructure that created a data dashboard for its LLCs. In addition, the Undergraduate Studies committee at the university conducts a review of all of its LLCs every four years.

Grogan College at the University of North Carolina at Greensboro (UNCG)

This program uses a comprehensive assessment design. At the foundational and formative assessment level, they conduct program-wide mid-semester feedback with their students, and the program chair also meets with the Grogan faculty every two to three weeks to discuss student feedback and check-in on how the students are progressing. For their summative assessment, UNCG's Residential College Office administers an exit survey to all of the second-year students who completed their capstones across all of their colleges. At the intermediate level, UNCG annually tracks the retention, persistence, and graduation rates of their LLC students. And, at the advanced level, they have intermittently used data from the National Survey of Student Engagement (NSSE) to inform their programming decisions.

The Grogan College staff have also used their assessment data comprehensively. Internally, student feedback has informed some curriculum changes. For example, Grogan's students indicated that they wanted more hands-on, real-world problems to engage with through internships. They also expressed a desire to perform more service in the local community. Subsequently, Grogan College created a 1-credit course to assist students in finding internships in their communities, and students who took the course could use their internship as the basis for their capstone project. Grogan's assessment data has also been used at the institutional level. Grogan regularly provides assessment information to the director of the residential colleges, who in turn includes the data in her annual report to the provost. The director also shares data/narratives from the LLC students to the UNCG marketing department so that LLC students' experiences are used on the campus's website and in various publications. Finally, as an expectation of their jobs, the UNCG LLC staff regularly present their assessment findings at local, regional, and national conferences and often include their students as co-presenters.

Hereford Residential College at the University of Virginia

This program conducts a variety of assessment and research projects. Hereford has student participants check-in to an event using a QR code in order to track usage. Students are incentivized to use the QR code so that they can earn points for their floors toward a series of prizes distributed at the end of the year. Each fall, Hereford administers an interest survey to both its 200 students and 20 faculty fellows. In both cases, the Hereford staff is interested in knowing what priorities the students and fellows have for programs, activities, and events so that they can tailor their programming accordingly throughout the academic year. The Hereford Student Senate collects formative data after each event from its student representatives, and logs in their meeting minutes any recommendations for improvement for the execution of the program in subsequent years.

Finally, in addition to its regular assessments, the Hereford staff conducted a sequential explanatory mixed-methods research study (Creswell & Plano Clark, 2011) on conditions in Hereford's environment that do or do not facilitate students' sense of belonging and well-being. The staff obtained Institutional Research Board approval for its survey instrument and focus group protocols in early Fall 2020. In late Fall 2020, the survey instrument was administered to all Hereford students, and obtained a 42.4% response rate that was largely representative of the residential college membership. In Spring 2021, the staff recruited 31 students from all four class years and organized a series of eight focus groups in the following homogeneous groupings: two groups of first-year/transfer students who took an introductory course; two groups of first-year/transfer students who did not take the course; two groups of returning second- through fourth-year students; and two groups of student leaders (RAs and Hereford Student Senators).

The results of the survey data revealed that, unsurprisingly, the returning second- through fourth-year students exhibited the strongest sense of belonging to Hereford College. Meanwhile, themes extracted from the focus group data showed that a combination of the physical, programmatic, social, and diverse human environments at Hereford contributed to students' sense of belonging. The fact that the College is situated on the edge of campus and is the furthest away from the center of grounds helped the Hereford students, who are physically separated from other social opportunities, find more kinship in their LLC. And, for some racially/ethnically underrepresented students, being further away from the dominant, predominantly White and upper-income peer culture of the center of campus helped to make Hereford a safe space for them to unwind.

Students with greater sense of belonging to the community not only attended more events but also felt as though they mattered to their peers when they did not attend an event and a hallmate would check in on them: "If I don't come to a program, people are like, 'Where are you? Or why weren't you there?' So it makes me feel like I belong to the community." Indeed, the combination of the natural setting in which Hereford is situated, the welcoming and friendly climate, and the diverse student membership facilitated a sense of belonging, especially among those who chose to return to live at Hereford in their second, third, and fourth years:

You get here and it's this community and this place where you think that we're going to talk about just trees [Hereford's logo is a tree]. It's actually really unique and nice, you know? It's really beautiful. It's really diverse. It's really a space where you can be yourself. And that's one of the reasons why I've always loved coming back here every year.

CONCLUSION

Assessment appears to remain one of the most challenging aspects of the LLC Best Practices Model. In addition to the revised Best Practices Model itself, in this chapter, we introduced two additional tools to assist practitioners in envisioning and enacting their own assessment plans: The Assessment typology and an LLC logic model. When considering their LLC's assessment needs, practitioners might consider beginning with the following questions:

1. What are your LLC's immediate assessment needs (i.e., what should be addressed first)?
2. What forms of assistance will your LLC need in order to conduct the assessments (e.g., obtaining institutional data, support with data collection, help with analysis)?
3. Who are your audiences (e.g., students, parents, institutional leaders) for your assessments and what will they be using the results to determine?
4. How can your LLC move from periodic to continuous assessment cycles?

REFERENCES

Council for the Advancement of Standards in Higher Education. (2023). *CAS professional standards for higher education* (11th version). Washington, DC: Author.

Creswell, J. W., & Plano Clark, V. L. (2011). *Designing and conducting mixed methods research* (2nd ed.). Los Angeles, CA: SAGE Publications.

Enhancing program performance with logic models. (2023, July 11). Retrieved from https://logicmodel.extension.wisc.edu/

Erkens, C. (2019). *The handbook for collaborative common assessments: Tools for design, delivery, and data analysis.* Bloomington, IN: Solution Tree Press.

Finley, A. (2019). *A comprehensive approach to assessment of high-impact practices* (Occasional Paper No. 41). Urbana, IL: University of Illinois and Indiana University, National Institute for Learning Outcomes Assessment (NILOA).

Upcraft, M. L., & Schuh, J. H. (1996). *Assessment in student affairs: A guide for practitioners.* San Francisco, CA: Jossey-Bass.

Wholey, J. S. (1979). *Evaluation: Promise and performance.* Washington, DC: Urban Institute.

Chapter 8

Best Practices in Living-Learning Communities: Integration and Communication

The "mortar" that holds the Best Practices Model elements together is integration and communication. Integration of all the elements discussed in previous chapters is essential for optimal implementation of living-learning communities (LLCs). When students see the connections between their academic and social experiences and the campus community, and when prospective students and families recognize the cohesive experience that is created through these programs, the LLC's value is clear. As noted by Inkelas et al. (2018), "… the purpose of an LLC is to provide its participants with a unified living and learning experience, where the program's theme permeates explicitly and seamlessly through all of its elements…" (p. 87). We remind readers that effective LLC programs are not simply a collection of individual elements but must include integration of both the experiences and the faculty and staff leadership to create a cohesive program. Effective communication is essential for these collaborative, intentional efforts to work – communication between and amongst those coordinating and leading LLCs, between leadership and students, and throughout the institution. In this chapter, we highlight the ways that integration and communication occur for quality LLCs (see the Integration and Communication Typology, Figure 8.2). We offer actual examples when possible and use a fictitious Political Science LLC to illustrate other elements as needed.

INTEGRATION OF THE LLC

As illustrated in Figure 8.1, all elements of the LLC must originate from the goals and objectives of Academic Affairs and Residence Life & Housing. There must be clear linkages back to the goals and objectives and between the other LLC features to create the best possible experience. About this integration, Inkelas et al. (2018) stated,

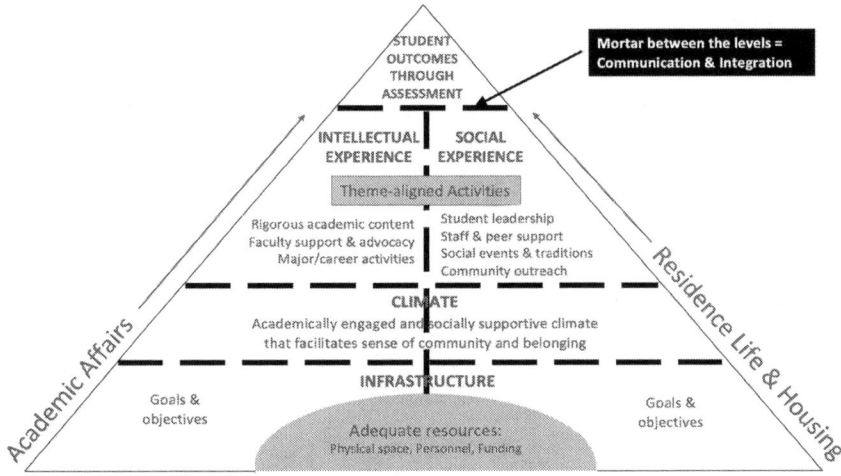

Figure 8.1 Integration and Communication in the Revised Best Practices Model.

> If all of the parts are present, but the parts do not make up a whole, then what emerges is a disparate set of activities that is not optimized for learning.... Without such integration, the LLC is really no better than a series of discrete and unrelated activities from which students can draw little meaning-making.
> (p. 24)

Additionally, integration of efforts on the part of LLC leadership is critical to weaving together the elements of the program. If the Residence Life & Housing staff and the faculty are not working in tandem, students may be confused about what to do and whether the activities and initiatives are part of the LLC, part of a class, or just part of the residence hall experience.

At the foundational level of the typology, LLCs are structured with all leadership participants focused on their specific area responsibilities. For example, a parallel partnership (Manning et al., 2014) could exist where Academic Affairs addresses curricular aspects and Student Affairs leads the cocurricular and housing elements of the LLC. Using this approach, Academic Affairs decides on and coordinates course- and other curriculum-related elements of the LLC, such as course syllabi, assignments and projects, and in some cases out-of-class activities that are specific to the course such as service learning events or field trips. RLH partners offer their expertise in the form of in-hall programming, which may include community building activities or programs coordinated and delivered by the residence hall staff (professionals as well as paraprofessionals) that are thematically connected to the LLC. In other words, both the Academic and Student Affairs stakeholders in the LLC are aligning their activities with the LLC's theme, but they are not integrating with one another. Using a Political Science LLC as an illustration, the academic leadership might include a course on U.S. voting rights and assign a project focused on increasing voter registration during an election year. The RLH staff may plan a viewing party of political debates that takes place within the LLC residence hall, possibly inviting a guest speaker to debrief with students after the event. Although all activities appear connected to the focus and objectives of the course, they are separate activities and students are left to integrate the information for themselves, something they may not realize they can and should do.

More ideal is planning and implementing the curriculum and co-curriculum with knowledge of potential conflicts and synergies at the intermediate level of the typology. At this level, both Academic Affairs and RLH LLC leadership inform each other of what is happening both inside and outside of the classroom, and efforts are made to ensure a level of coordination, although each may still be "staying in their lane" with regard to involvement in in- or out-of-the-classroom activities. Faculty may be aware of activities and remind students in class that an activity is both occurring and related to the LLC theme, while RLH staff may be aware of an assignment that students have in class and capitalize on that, as well as mention the connection, in an out-of-class activity they organize. In the Political Science LLC example, RLH leadership would have access to the course syllabus so that they could plan activities directly related to the course objectives and plans, and be able to coordinate activities so that they followed the syllabus schedule. Additionally, Academic Affairs leadership along with RLH and other student affairs professionals would communicate dates/times/locations of events and activities, perhaps creating a shared calendar for continued planning.

Advanced level LLCs are ones in which all elements are planned and implemented collaboratively and seamlessly. Students in such an LLC likely would not see their in-class experiences as separate from their out-of-class LLC experiences. Faculty teaching their LLC course(s) would be involved in, or at minimum informed of, out-of-class LLC activities, allowing them to reference such experiences in class to aid students in connecting the various elements of the LLC for a holistic experience. Faculty may also be participating in the activities with the students and RLH staff. RLH and other student affairs professionals would be positioned to do the same – remind students of course-related materials and how their activities illustrate and connect to their studies. Ideally, the academic and residence hall experiences might be co-facilitated by Academic and Student Affairs professionals collaboratively. Returning to our Political Science LLC example, the course instructor and the residence hall director might regularly meet and discuss class activities in order to plan complimentary out-of-class experiences that both may facilitate or participate in as leaders.

This integration, whether it is foundational, intermediate, or advanced, is not possible without sound communication amongst all those involved. "The academic affairs and RLH professional staffs must be knowledgeable about each other's roles in the LLC, as integration is impossible without regular and effective communication" (Inkelas et al., 2018, p. 84). Next, we discuss communication as an important aspect of the LLC that cements other LLC elements in place.

COMMUNICATION

Communication can take many formats, from electronic information made generally available or specifically sent to LLC students, staff, faculty, and others at the institution, to flyers hung in the residence hall, to face-to-face communication through meetings or class announcements. While it's easy to jump quickly to consideration of electronic communication, it is important to remember the value of word-of-mouth and face-to-face communication, which can facilitate connections and potentially deepen relationships.

Perhaps because institutions provide email addresses for students, faculty, and staff and expect them to check their campus email for general information, email is probably the most commonly used communication approach. While results from one study indicated that more than 80% of college-going students reported checking their email one or more times a day (EAB, 2019), another study of college students at one institution indicated that 54% of respondents shared that they don't regularly read emails from the institution (EAB, 2020). Effective ways to get students' attention and encourage them to open emails include using catchy subject lines that are clear to students, leading with one "Call to Action" in your subject line, and conveying a sense of urgency if there is one. Additionally, making messages personal by addressing the student as "you" and eliminating the confusing higher education jargon can lead to success in reaching students (EAB, 2020).

Websites are a valuable location for LLC information that those seeking information can visit first to find out about activities and events. These also serve as an important recruitment tool, communicating to potential students and families the value as well as the specifics of LLCs. According to a 2019 EAB study, 76.3% of high school student respondents indicated that they would search the college's website if they had a general question about the institution, suggesting that this communication format continues to be a relied-upon source of information. LLCs should have up-to-date information available on their websites for both recruitment of new students and information for those students currently involved in the LLC.

Given students' prolific use of social media, having a GroupMe, Instagram, TikTok, or other currently popular accounts for the program can assist in getting important information out to those who need it. Particularly as it relates to transitions to a new location, social media can assist students in forming a new social community (Waite & Wheeler, 2020). Using such sites to supplement communication and reinforce messages as opposed to serving as the primary mode of communication is recommended (Wesley & Dunlap, 2019). Questions may arise about who controls the social media for the LLC — is it the faculty/staff leadership or is it the students? Faculty and staff may feel less knowledgeable about social media use and see this as an opportunity to capitalize on students' general understanding of the various platforms their peers appreciate. Ahlquist (2018) recommends utilizing student influencers, students who are known on campus and active on social media who can serve as connectors. Use of a student social media influencer doesn't mean that faculty and staff step away from managing social media but involves featuring these known students and utilizing the influence they have on campus. Other recommendations for student influencers include having diverse representation, outlined job expectations, and clear messaging to viewers that the students are employed in this role (Rolfs et al., 2019). When LLC students create the content, it gives them ownership (Waite & Wheeler, 2020) and may result in greater investment in the LLC. However, training is necessary for such a role (Rolfs et al., 2019). The #YourRedbirdLife Student Influencer program at Illinois State University is a good example of such a program (Rolfs et al., 2019).

Wesley and Dunlap (2019) recommend informing students about how the institution will communicate with them so students are prepared for information to reach them in certain ways. LLCs should do the same. If the plan is to primarily communicate LLC information to participants via email, through the course management system, or through a platform like Slack, students must be clearly alerted to that communication plan. For emails, the LLC might choose a consistent subject heading to signal to students that the information pertains to the program, particularly as students may be receiving other non-LLC information from these faculty and staff. Wesley and Dunlap (2019) also encourage involving students in determining the communication approaches, stating "Involving students in the development of communication strategies is essential, as sometimes student affairs professionals' perceptions about student preferences can miss the mark" (p. 10). They also suggest gathering feedback from students about the communication approach to determine what strategies work. Regarding text messaging, Wesley and Dunlap noted a concern about equity issues as they relate to phone and data plan costs, which could be prohibitive for some students and result in them not receiving important LLC information.

Because LLCs are partnerships, there are multiple stakeholders who need to be informed. Gruenewald and Brooke (2007) highlighted the importance of determining who to include in learning community communication networks. While the partnership between the RLH staff and faculty LLC leaders is obvious, other important partnerships for communication might include admissions and the university marketing team so that an effective branding campaign can exist. Understanding the different work of the subcultures involved in these collaborative efforts matters – "… we must also openly acknowledge differences and respect the diversity of subcultures of the university in order to facilitate open communication" (Gruenewald & Brooke, 2007, p. 41). Transparency about roles and responsibilities within the leadership group also is recommended for effective collaboration (Inkelas et al., 2018).

Communication with Students about LLC Initiatives

Foundational level communication with students about LLC initiatives is limited and siloed. Students learn about LLC activities from the coordinating entity, with academic information conveyed by Academic Affairs and cocurricular information shared by RLH and other Student Affairs professionals. At this level, it is likely that both academic and RLH staff trust that they are each doing what needs to be done, but communication amongst faculty and staff is limited, which can result in inefficiencies as well as duplication of efforts. At one institution, a current challenge is that RLH staff are trying to engage with faculty to do academic programming while faculty teaching the LLC course are doing similar work. This can limit integration and also result in competing activities, such as the example Political Science LLC having a guest speaker in the hall for an evening event on the same night that the Political Science department has sponsored an event that students are encouraged to attend.

The intermediate level is similar to the foundational level; however, faculty and staff may communicate more amongst each other about what each is planning. Students and LLC leadership are still informed about LLC initiatives by the coordinating entity, suggesting separation in the activities. In our Political Science LLC example, the staff may consult the faculty about appropriate speakers; inform them of the date, time, and location of the event; and invite them to attend; in this instance, the staff would provide primary communication with students about the event. Or the faculty may be planning a panel of experts, inform the staff, request assistance in securing space in the residence hall for the event, and communicate with students in the course about the event. In each case, faculty and staff maintain primary ownership over the initiative they coordinated but seek some minor assistance from their LLC partner.

At the advanced level, LLC faculty and staff coordinate communication about LLC initiatives and provide unified messages to students. This requires a team approach that includes sharing information about all aspects of the LLC amongst the leadership so that coordinated communication can occur. Such an approach typically requires regular meetings of the leadership team. One activity in which LLC leadership might engage together is the creation of an LLC calendar of events, activities, and deadlines that is shared with all LLC participants – students, faculty, and staff. LLC leadership could also use tools such as Microsoft Teams or a Google Drive folder to share information amongst the leaders. Both Academic Affairs and RLH staff may have access to the learning management system for the course and be able to add announcements and information there as well. The Political Science LLC example might include a shared weekly email update to students or shared announcements that are communicated to students both in class, through the LMS, as well as through the residence hall staff. Waite and Wheeler (2020) noted that using social media instead of the LMS may be more familiar and less formal for students, potentially garnering more attention from them. At Hereford Residential College at the University of Virginia, the weekly "Hereford Happenings" email includes announcements about upcoming events as well as a weekly mindfulness tip (e.g., short meditation, breathing exercises, coloring) since mindfulness is one of the college's primary foci. Similarly, the Gemstones Program at the University of Maryland uses a weekly newsletter to convey LLC information. Such a coordinated process offers the benefit of decreasing the volume of emails students receive (Wesley & Dunlap, 2019) and provides a unified message.

Communication across LLC Leadership

Communication about the LLC amongst the faculty and RLH professional staff may occur electronically or in-person, and in either format the communication can range from strictly informing colleagues about what is occurring to planning LLC initiatives together. Decisions about a communication process that works for all involved is critical. Whether and how often face-to-face meetings occur, who schedules those meetings, who convenes the meetings, etc. should be discussed by LLC leadership, regardless of where the program is on the typology.

Rudimentary communication across LLC leadership involves student affairs staff communicating information to other student affairs colleagues and faculty communicating LLC information to their departmental colleagues. This foundational level approach allows both leadership groups to ensure that their area is informed about the activities of the LLC. Grills et al. (2012) reinforced the need for this communication to ensure that faculty LLC leaders' departmental colleagues are aware of what is occurring in the program so they can contribute to making it more effective. Student affairs staff are unlikely to have the same access to these faculty members, so LLC faculty leaders must facilitate that communication. The same is true for Student Affairs professionals, whose access to their colleagues is greater than the LLC faculty leaders' access. However, with separate communication, messaging may be inconsistent or differently timed such that student affairs staff or faculty are not aware of the other's efforts in a timely fashion. This separation can also lead to confusion and questions from students that leaders are not able to answer. For example, the Political Science LLC guest speaker arranged by the RLH staff may be highlighted at a staff meeting or weekly update to student affairs professional staff. However, if faculty are not clear on the details and students ask questions about the event in class or if they ask other faculty in the department, those individuals may not be able to provide information, suggesting that the experience is less connected to their academics and the LLC.

At the intermediate level of communication, student affairs staff communicate LLC information to divisional colleagues and faculty more broadly while LLC faculty communicate program information to college/school (or equivalent) and colleagues in the division of Academic Affairs. Similar to the foundational level, intermediate level communication has separate messaging but reaches beyond divisional or college/school boundaries. At this level, faculty and student affairs professionals keep both their immediate colleagues and each other informed such that both can easily access the information if asked. This might include faculty informing the hall director or the Student Affairs LLC leader of activities with a request that they forward the information to their colleagues, and vice versa. The hall director would contact the faculty member for the Political Science LLC to let them know about the guest speaker, for example, and ask the faculty member to share the invitation with the rest of the Political Science department to expand the program's reach.

Advanced-level communication includes a uniform communication plan across the university that highlights the importance of both Student and Academic Affairs. Student Affairs staff and faculty work together to coordinate information-sharing for the entire institution. This would likely be for all institutional LLCs. A monthly or semesterly newsletter is one option and could include highlights from LLC initiatives and events along with information about upcoming activities. LLC leadership might also work with the university marketing team to feature LLC programming in university-wide news items. In our Political Science LLC example, the guest speaker, panel of experts, service learning activities, and the like might be featured in the newsletter along with a schedule of upcoming events. This approach requires advance planning on the part of the LLC leadership.

Communication at the Institutional Level

Communication to the rest of the campus community about the LLCs is important if the goal is to institutionalize these programs. When those outside of the LLC are informed, they can share information with others that might aid in recruitment, programming efforts, national rankings, and other beneficial outcomes.

No communication about LLC initiatives exists in formal institutional communications at the foundational level. This may indicate that LLCs are departmental/divisional initiatives as opposed to institutionally supported efforts. Upper-level administrators may have little or no knowledge of the programs, making it impossible for them to champion these initiatives.

Intermediate level institutional communication about LLC initiatives happens on relevant committees (undergraduate education, division of student affairs). Champions at the departmental/divisional levels inform others about LLCs when the opportunity is present, but no mechanism is in place for communication at an institutional level. Under these circumstances, if a committee doesn't have an LLC faculty or staff member on the committee, no information will be passed on to colleagues, leaving areas of campus uninformed and unable to support the program. For our example Political Science LLC, the faculty leader of the program may be a member of the Undergraduate Curriculum Committee and able to share information with committee colleagues about the LLC, expanding the knowledge about the program to other parts of campus, while the Director of Residence Life may participate on the New Student Transition Committee and share with colleagues the transition benefits noted through an assessment of the LLC that can lead to interest in creating additional LLCs. Without these LLC leaders on the committees, at the intermediate level of institutional communication this information would not surface within the contexts of those groups.

At the advanced level, communication about LLC initiatives is part of formal senior level communication about educational quality. LLCs may be specifically noted in the strategic plan as it is under the "Thrive" theme of the Boldly Elon strategic plan at Elon University (Elon University, n.d.). A campus committee with representatives from Student and Academic Affairs may oversee LLCs and disseminate information about these programs through regular meetings and other university communication channels. These individuals could also make a specific effort or have an expectation to pass on information in other settings to campus constituents. Iowa State University offers such an example, with a Learning Community Advisory Committee, comprised of faculty and staff, serving as a main communication mechanism for learning community information for the campus (Gruenewald & Brooke, 2007).

Integration of all parts of the LLC (both program planning and execution) spotlights the connection of the various parts of the program. Without integration, there may be in- and out-of-class elements that are based on the same theme, but students are unlikely to make the connections, eliminating the uniqueness of the LLC experience. Communication – amongst LLC students, faculty, and staff as well as beyond the program to the division, college/school, and institution – demonstrates the interconnections of the various elements and illuminates what the program provides, allowing the entire institution to play a role in the program's success.

Programs in their early stages may be starting at the foundational level of the typology, while working toward more intermediate and advanced elements of integration and communication. This makes sense since there is usually a building stage for LLCs, starting at the departmental level and eventually gaining institutional recognition. As readers peruse the typology (Figure 8.2), consider these questions about your LLC:

1. How will you ensure that students recognize the connection between their in- and out-of-class LLC activities?
2. What does each LLC partner bring to the team (e.g., strengths, skills) that the team can capitalize on for integration of LLC elements?
3. What are the most effective ways to communicate with students at your institution?
4. What resources do you have for communication? For example, can you hire a student to manage LLC social media accounts?
5. How will LLC faculty and RLH staff stay informed about what each is doing within the LLC?
6. How will you get information out to the broader campus community about LLC initiatives, successes, and opportunities for their contributions to and collaborations with the LLC?

Attribute	Foundational	Intermediate	Advanced
Integration of LLC	Parallel partnership exists where academic affairs address curricular aspects and student affairs leads the co-curricular and housing aspects of LLC	Curriculum and co-curriculum are planned and implemented with knowledge of potential conflicts and synergies	All aspects of the curriculum and co-curriculum are planned and implemented seamlessly across academic and student affairs
Communication with students about LLC initiatives	Students are informed by coordinating entity about LLC initiatives, faculty and staff communication amongst each other is limited	Students and LLC leadership are informed by coordinating entity about LLC initiatives	All LLC faculty and staff coordinate communication about LLC initiatives and provide unified message to students
Communication across LLC leadership	Student affairs staff communicate LLC information to departmental colleagues. Faculty communicate LLC information to departmental colleagues	Student affairs staff communicate LLC information to divisional colleagues and faculty more broadly. Faculty communicate LLC information to college/school (or equivalent) and colleagues in the division of student affairs	Uniform communication plan across the university that highlights the importance of both student and academic affairs
Communication at the institutional level	No communication about LLC initiatives exists in formal institutional communications	Communication about LLC initiatives happens on relevant committees (undergraduate education, division of student affairs)	Communication about LLC initiatives is part of formal senior level communication about educational quality

Figure 8.2 Integration and Communication Typology.

REFERENCES

Ahlquist, J. (2018, October 11). *Advanced social media strategies for student affairs*. www.josieahlquist.com; Advanced Social Media Strategies for Student Affairs – Josie Ahlquist.

EAB. (2019). *Trends identified in the 2019 EAB student communication survey*. EMS-08272019StudentCommSlides-PDF.pdf (eab.com).

EAB. (2020). *Optimizing your student communications success strategy: Toolkit from "breaking through the student communications barrier."* How to Optimize Your Student Communications Strategy | EAB.

Elon University. (n.d.). *Boldly Elon Theme 2: Thrive*. Elon, NC: Elon University/Boldly Elon/Thrive.

Grills, C. N., Fingerhut, A. W., Thadani, V., & Machon, R. A. (2012, Winter). Residential learning communities centered with a discipline: The Psychology Early Awareness Program. In K. Buch & K. E. Barron (Eds.), *Discipline-centered learning communities: Creating connections among students, faculty, and curricula* (New Directions for Teaching and Learning, p. 132). Hoboken, NJ: Wiley.

Gruenewald, D., & Brooke, C. (2007). Working together from the ground up. In B. L. Smith, L. B. Williams & others (Eds.), *Learning communities and student affairs partnerships: Partnering for powerful learning* (pp. 35–46). Learning Communities & Educational Reform, Fall, Olympia, WA: The Evergreen State College, Washington Center for Improving the Quality of Undergraduate Education.

Inkelas, K. K., Jessup-Anger, J., Benjamin, M., & Wawrzynski, M. (2018). *Living-learning communities that work: A research-based model for design, delivery, and assessment*. Sterling, VA: Stylus Publishing, LLC.

Manning, K., Kinzie, J., & Schuh, J. H. (2014). *One size does not fit all: Traditional and innovative models of student affairs practice* (2nd ed.). New York: Routledge.

Rolfs, M., Ahlquist, J., & Johnson, L. (2019, Fall). Influencer marketing for student affairs. *NASPA Leadership Exchange, 17*, 38–39.

Waite, B. C., & Wheeler, D. A. (2020). *Social media for student affairs in #highereducation: Trends, challenges, and opportunities*. Lanham, MD: Rowman & Littlefield.

Wesley, A., & Dunlap, J. (2019). *Five things student affairs professionals should know about managing email communication with students*. Washington, DC: NASPA: Student Affairs Administrators in Higher Education.

Chapter 9

Final Thoughts on Living-Learning Communities in Practice

FROM STATUS QUO TO ASPIRATION

Our aim in writing this book was to use the revised Best Practices Model (BPM) as a framework for illustrating examples of living-learning communities (LLCs) in practice. In addition, we sought to help readers realize the potential of their LLCs by offering the typologies and logic model. Readers of the revised BPM, examples, and typologies provided in this book may be wondering if it is actually possible to achieve the most advanced levels of the model and typologies. We identified our original BPM (Inkelas et al., 2018) as a blueprint for effective LLCs. But as anyone who has ever built a house or been involved in a building project knows, blueprints are often the ideal and the end result may be a variation on that ideal. Our revised BPM is a similar blueprint that highlights different stages of LLC development. As such, the revised BPM is aspirational, with the LLC characteristics in the advanced column of the typology as high-level goals. Although we believe that all LLCs can achieve the foundational level, the intermediate and advanced levels offer direction for continued LLC innovation. There is no perfect model or way to organize and coordinate LLCs, but our hope is that the revised BPM, typologies, and institutional examples offer guidance and options that may be adapted differently depending on institutional goals and contexts.

The logic model we introduced in Chapter 7 may be another source of inspiration for LLC administrators wishing to initiate, enhance, or revitalize their LLCs. Just as the typologies offer ways to envision more complex and distinctive LLCs, the logic model expands upon this notion by connecting the work of LLCs with their hypothesized student outcomes. Moreover, the student outcomes are presented in increasingly nuanced ways that differentiate between immediate, direct effects of LLC participation (i.e., short-term outcomes) and outcomes that evolve over time and further reflection (medium- and long-term outcomes). Similar to the flexible philosophy behind the design of the typologies, there is no expectation that LLC administrators should use the revised BPM, typologies, and logic model to design comprehensive assessment plans all at once. In keeping with our house blueprint metaphor, instead, LLC practitioners can think of these assessment tools as ways to remodel specific portions of the home instead of building the whole house from scratch. Using the revised BPM, LLC staff can identify which portions of their communities (aka houses) need additional attention and improvement. They can then use the typologies to see how they can improve those parts of their communities from foundational to intermediate to advanced levels. Finally, they can use a logic model to empirically test how these improvements may have impacted their participants' outcomes – outcomes tailored to their particular programs and students. This process will necessarily take time and long-term planning. However, if done well, an assessment plan with this level of sophistication will be second-to-none, which will ultimately illustrate whether these initiatives are enhancing the undergraduate experience, and, if so, how.

THE ROLE OF LLCS IN IMPROVING THE STUDENT EXPERIENCE

As LLC administrators continue to refine their LLCs, it is important to situate these initiatives alongside the original and contemporary aims of these communities. Although originally designed as a way to cohere students' undergraduate experience (Jessup-Anger, 2015), today LLCs are more commonly associated with the "learning community" High-Impact Practice (HIP), which is one of several experiences (i.e. internships, capstone experiences, undergraduate research, etc.) that are particularly successful in promoting student engagement. These types of engagement experiences may play a key role in helping to achieve the transformative learning that students, faculty, and administrators strive for in postsecondary education (Kuh, 2008; Zilvinskis et al., 2022).

Certainly, learning communities without the residential element may offer many of the structures and opportunities available in LLCs (as made evident in the typologies throughout the book); however, the creation of communities within residence halls offers students the benefit of environmental press – the social and cultural cues within the environment that encourage students to adapt to that environment (Strange & Banning, 2015). In an LLC, this press favors academic and social integration, as fostered through the climate (addressed in Chapter 4), intellectual (addressed in Chapter 5), and social experiences (addressed in Chapter 6) of the LLC. This press results in greater time-on-task, or at least greater time in recognition of students' intellectual focus. When students are clustered together around a common intellectual interest in a space that includes indicators of that common interest and the goals of the program (such as group study space, art, or other visuals that reflect the theme), they can more regularly support each other in their intellectual pursuits as well as through the challenges that are common in the college experience. Particularly on a residential campus, where peers are engaged outside of class often more than in classrooms, LLCs are an effective way to promote coherent, integrative, and transformative learning.

As we addressed in *Living-Learning Communities that Work* (Inkelas et al., 2018), LLCs also work effectively when integrated with other HIPs. Kinzie (2012) argued that participation in multiple HIPs can be more beneficial than participation in one, and since then, other scholars (i.e. Finley & Kuh, 2016) highlighted possibilities of embedding other high-impact practices (such as first-year seminars, service learning, and capstone experiences) into LLCs to deepen the impact of these initiatives. As administrators grapple with which HIPs to focus their time and limited resources on, it may be important to consider when, in a student's time in college, they should encounter HIPs and for what purpose. Many LLCs coincide with students' first year, which is a time fraught with anxiety about their transition to college. LLCs can help a student to feel socially and academically integrated to the university and cultivate a sense of purpose (Jessup-Anger, 2012). Of course, these outcomes should be clear from the outset, with the goals and objectives of both academic affairs and housing and residence life aligned with this aim.

In addition to considering whether and how to situate LLCs within the undergraduate experience, administrators' attention should be increasingly focused on the quality of implementation of these initiatives. Mayhew (2019) deemed highly impactful practitioners' implementation of HIPs as central to the success of these initiatives. In their ten-year retrospectives on HIPs, Kuh and colleagues (2017) cautioned university leaders to work to ensure the quality of these initiatives by attending to the educational practices undergirding them. Assessment is critical to determine if an initiative is, in fact, high impact, and is "what will separate the committed practitioners from the casual adopters" (Finley, 2019, p. 4). Using the revised BPM as a framework and guiding implementation through the use of the typologies and logic model can aid in moving LLCs from casual adoption to full implementation.

To ensure that LLCs truly improve undergraduates' experience in college, LLC practitioners need to attend to equity in addition to quality. Zilvinskis et al. (2022) emphasize the importance of advocating for equity in high-impact practices, highlighting in particular that practitioners have known since the introduction of the high-impact monniker, and have had confirmed by recent NSSE reports, that first-generation and African American students are least likely to participate in HIPs. However, Kinzie et al. (2021) noted that racially minoritized students who participated in high-impact practices felt positive about the broader connections and networks that resulted from their participation. Through theme-aligned activities and the social experiences, some of these connections and networks may be established within LLCs. Thus, it is critical to situate equity as a precursor and central value in the development and sustainability of LLCs. To do so, LLC administrators must attend to barriers of participation.

Barriers to participation in LLCs may exist for students if there are costs associated with the program. Aiming to keep these costs low or offering scholarships for students under a particular income threshold are ways to address the cost dimension. Another potential barrier is not having sufficient knowledge to apply. Targeted outreach aimed at students who have historically not participated in LLCs (namely, students of color, first-generation students, and low-income students) is one way to begin to address inequity in access which is important – as these students, when in LLCs, often have stronger outcomes than their peers (Inkelas & Associates, 2007; Nosaka & Novak, 2014). Perhaps the most successful way to address inequity is to scale up LLC efforts so that all first-year students living on campus are required to live in an LLC. This attention to scale is a dimension identified by Kinzie et al. (2021) as important for ensuring quality in HIP implementation. Although doing so would require a substantial institutional investment, the result may be a student population poised for successful retention and completion. This approach is well suited for a campus-serving traditional-age first-year students; however, it excludes older students, who are likely not living on campus. For those students, other versions of learning communities and other high-impact practices may be more suited for their circumstances.

These non-residential programs share many similarities with LLCs, and have as a central element the goal of bringing students together around common interests. Learning communities often include common courses among a cohort of students, also possible through LLCs. Both types of learning communities may also sponsor out-of-class activities related to the course content or a theme. Both may employ peer mentors, include service learning opportunities, be part of a larger first-year experience program, and/or incorporate team-based learning. The National Learning Community Program Directory, hosted by The Washington Center at Evergreen State College, offers a great deal of information about all learning community types (National Learning Community Program Directory | The Washington Center (evergreen.edu)).

THE FUTURE FOR LLCS IN AMERICAN HIGHER EDUCATION AS SEEN THROUGH THE COVID-19 PANDEMIC

The onset of the COVID-19 pandemic illustrated both strengths and potential vulnerabilities in the LLC model. After years of questions and suspicion regarding the value of in-person learning at the collegiate level, the arrival of the COVID-19 pandemic forced colleges and universities to pivot online virtually overnight. Although some advocates of shifting postsecondary institutions to online formats saw this disruption as an opportunity to finally illustrate the benefit of the online model (Gallagher & Palmer, 2020), emerging research from the pandemic illustrates that students caught up in the crisis faced tremendous difficulty in their courses (Gillis & Krull, 2020), emotional well-being (Soria & Horgos, 2021), and in their lives generally (Glantsman et al., 2022).

Students enrolled in well-functioning LLCs, perhaps more so than the general residential population, had relationships in place with faculty and staff that enabled them to continue the engagement recognized as beneficial to students' learning experiences, or at the very least, provided them with the requisite connections to reach out when facing difficulties. Benjamin et al. (2020) noted benefits of learning communities that included "providing a coherent, interdisciplinary space for intellectual engagement," "leveraging relationships among faculty, staff and students to provide support," and "connecting students with their institution" (1–2), all of which continued to be important elements of LLCs during the pandemic, and may have been helpful to students as they navigated the crisis.

Efforts to provide these coherences and relationships during the COVID-19 upheaval provided LLC administrators with valuable lessons that can be incorporated into current LLC work. LLC administrators faced constraints during the pandemic that ironically were a product of their strengths. The most obvious was that these initiatives rely on relationships to create environmental press (Strange & Banning, 2015) and build the sense of belonging (Moore, 2023) necessary to forge their transformative effect. These relationships had to be developed differently in light of the shuttered classrooms and closed or severely restricted residence halls.

Thus, recruiting students into LLCs and helping to foster relationships happened differently during the acute phase of the pandemic. Virtual coffee chats with LLC and learning community administrators revealed anecdotes illustrating how LLC practitioners used meeting technology (Zoom, MS Teams) for communication to a greater degree with LLC participants as a way to check-in and connect with them when face-to-face modes of communication were inaccessible. In addition, they used technology to a greater degree in community building with new LLC participants—from orientation efforts to welcome week activities, especially in the fall of 2020 when opportunities for large gatherings may have been restricted. LLC administrators reported a positive response to such outreach, suggesting that these types of connections with students might continue beyond the pandemic as a way to build community before students are even on campus. Such efforts can connect students both with the institution and with each other and "early and continued outreach can help students feel comfortable committing to an institution and remaining in school" (Benjamin et al., 2020, p. 2).

Another constraint that was brought to the forefront during the pandemic was the limits of administrator bandwidth and resources. The COVID-19 pandemic brought about feelings of burnout across multiple sectors of modern society, with those on the front lines of the crisis, including medical providers, educators, and front-line support staff, shouldering a heavy burden. LLC administrators, who often take on LLC responsibilities in addition to other academic or administrative roles, saw their work shift from community building to crisis management overnight. These other responsibilities sometimes overtook the important work of LLC administration, illustrating the small margin upon which these communities are operating. An important lesson from the pandemic is to continue to resource these communities in a way that ensures their sustainability in the face of crisis. Although, hopefully, the COVID-19 pandemic is a once-in-a-lifetime event, there will surely be other crises that draw attention away from the important work being done in LLCs. Resourcing these initiatives sustainably will ensure they are not one crisis away from extinction.

Worldwide pandemics notwithstanding, the living-learning concept has been in existence for centuries on college campuses and their staying power is no doubt related to their ability to integrate those beneficial aspects of the college experience that have also stood the test of time: engagement with faculty, interactions with peers, friendships deepened through shared interests and bonds, and a living environment that is welcoming and supportive. While no one knows what the future of American higher education holds, some incarnation of LLCs will likely continue to exist because they embody these timeless characteristics.

REFERENCES

Benjamin, M., Gebauer, R., Godowski, J., Graziano, J., Henscheid, J. M., Jessup-Anger, J., Kinzie, J., Inkelas, K. K., Lundeen, S., Metzker, J., & Sperry, R. (2020, October). The promise of learning communities in a reimagined undergraduate education. *The Toolbox, 19*(2). National Resource Center for the First-Year Experience and Students in Transition. Retrieved from https://issuu.com/nrcpubs/docs/toolbox_19.2?fr=sMmY5NDQ5NjgONA

Finley, A. (2019). *A comprehensive approach to assessment of high-impact practices* (Occasional Paper No. 41). Urbana, IL: University of Illinois and Indiana University, National Institute for Learning Outcomes Assessment (NILOA).

Finley, A., & Kuh, G. D. (2016). The case for connecting first-year seminars and learning communities. In L. C. Schmidt & J. Graziano (Eds.), *Building synergy for high-impact educational initiatives: First-year seminars and learning communities* (pp. 3–18). Columbia, SC: University of South Carolina, National Resource Center for the First-Year Experience and Students in Transition.

Gallagher, S., & Palmer, J. (2020, September 29). The pandemic pushed universities online. The change was long overdue. *Harvard Business Review*. Retrieved from https://hbr.org/2020/09/the-pandemic-pushed-universities-online-the-change-was-long-overdue

Gillis, A., & Krull, L. M. (2020). COVID-19 remote learning transition in spring 2020: Class structures, student perceptions, and inequality in college courses. *Teaching Sociology, 48*(4), 283–299.

Glantsman, O., McGarity-Palmer, R., Swanson, H. L., Carroll, J. T., Zinter, K. E., Lancaster, K. M., & Berardi, L. (2022). Risk of food and housing insecurity among college students during the COVID-19 pandemic, *Journal of Community Psychology, 50*, 2726–2745.

Inkelas, K. K., & Associates. (2007). *The national study of living-learning programs: 2007 report of findings*. College Park, MD: The University of Maryland.

Inkelas, K. K., Jessup-Anger, J., Benjamin, M., & Wawrzynski, M. (2018). *Living-learning communities that work: A research-based model for design, delivery, and assessment*. Sterling, VA: Stylus Publishing, LLC.

Jessup-Anger, J. E. (2012). Examining how residential colleges inspire the life of the mind. *Review of Higher Education, 35*(3), 431–462.

Jessup-Anger, J. (2015). Theoretical foundations of learning communities. In M. Benjamin (Ed.), *New directions for student services* (pp. 17–27). San Francisco, CA: Jossey-Bass.

Kinzie, J. (2012). Optimizing high impact practices in the senior year. In M. S. Hunter, J. R. Keup, J. Kinzie, & H. Maietta (Eds.), *The senior year: Culminating experiences and transitions* (pp. 71–90). Columbia, SC: University of South Carolina, National Resource Center for the First-Year Experience and Students in Transition.

Kinzie, J., Silberstein, S., McCormick, A. C., Gonyea, R. M., & Dugan, B. (2021). Centering racially minoritized student voices in high-impact practices. *Change: The Magazine for Higher Learning, 53*(4), 6–14.

Kuh, G. D. (2008). *High-impact educational practices: What they are, who has access to them, and why they matter*. Washington, DC: Association of American Colleges and Universities.

Kuh, G. D., O'Donnell, K., Schneider, C. G. (2017). HIPs at ten. *Change: The Magazine of Higher Learning, 49*(5), 8–16. doi: 10.1080;00091383.2017.1366805

Mayhew, M. J. (2019, October). *Empirically substantiating claims about "high impact" practices in teaching and learning*. Presented at the Canadian Institutional Research and Planning Association, Montreal, Canada.

Moore, J. L. (2023). *Key practices for fostering engaged learning: A guide for faculty and staff*. New York: Routledge.

Nosaka, T., & Novak, H. (2014). Against the odds: The impact of the Key Communities at Colorado State University on retention and graduation for historically underrepresented students. *Learning Communities Research and Practice, 2*(2), 3. Retrieved from https://airtable.com/appXYu1qwxpyPwqH6/shrn4SLzHJ1M-r62XB/tblTC2OhqfZt567Po/viweB8XZL6F5tsyGe/rec4pcoWIewFYQvfk/fldSRfESKfQ8pms3w/attsx3XPm7OJMjvqA

Soria, K. M., & Horgos, B. (2021). Factors associated with college students' mental health during the COVID-19 pandemic. *Journal of College Student Development, 62*(2), 236–242.

Strange, C. C., & Banning, J. H. (2015). *Designing for learning: Creating campus environments for student success.* San Francisco, CA: Jossey-Bass.

Zilvinskis, J., Kinzie, J., Daday, J., O'Donnell, K., & Vande Zande, C. (2022). *Delivering on the promise of high-impact practices: Research and models for achieving equity, fidelity, and scale.* Sterling, VA: Stylus.

Afterword

It bears repeating in this final section of a book that seeks to enhance living-learning communities that living-learning communities (LLCs) have many educational benefits and proven outcomes. As one of the oldest forms of what are now labeled High-Impact Practices (HIPs), learning communities have been a part of American colleges and universities since the colonial era. As a purposeful approach to integrate curricular, cocurricular, and residential components, LLCs foster collaboration among students, faculty, and staff and enhance students' academic and social development. They positively contribute to persistence, student engagement, and cognitive gains and are credited with increasing community, sense of belonging, and providing a smoother transition and supportive experience for a more diverse student population (Dunn & Dean, 2013; Inkelas et al., 2018; Inkelas & Soldner, 2011; Mayhew et al., 2016; Strayhorn, 2023). Without a doubt, the benefits of LLCs are robust. Yet, as this book so clearly explicates, LLCs can aspire to so much more and they deserve greater investment by colleges and universities.

When I wrote the Foreword to *Living-Learning Communities that Work: A Research-Based Model for Design, Delivery, and Assessment* in 2018, I extolled the virtues of learning communities and praised their potential for enhancing collegiate quality and increasing student success. The original Living-Learning Best Practices Model (BPM) provided a solid framework for taking stock of practice and for designing maximally effective LLCs. Since the 2018 publication, the authors have persisted in advancing their living learning community research and thoughtfully revising their best practices model to offer an even more instructive blueprint for enhancing LLCs. Authors Karen Kurotsuchi Inkelas, Mimi Benjamin, and Jody Jessup-Anger, and their colleagues who participated in the Center for Engaged Learning research seminar on Residential Learning Communities at Elon University, and all the living-learning practitioners who offered feedback on the model and shared in this study, deserve our profound thanks for persevering and extending the reach of living-learning community research and practice.

AFTERWORD

This book, *Living-Learning Communities in Practice: A Guide for Creating, Maintaining, and Sustaining Effective Programs in Higher Education*, takes living-learning community research and practice to the next level. The revised model debuts at an opportune moment for higher education. Interest continues to grow in making practices such as learning communities known to contribute to student success a guaranteed experience at colleges and universities. Investments in the refinements that make these experiences maximally effective are also needed. Even more, following unprecedented disruption in colleges and universities caused by the COVID-19 pandemic that kept us socially distant, and the parallel instances of racial injustice that further exposed systemic racism in higher education, there is tremendous need to foster supportive communities that are more equitable and inclusive.

By producing a thoroughly researched, workshopped, applied, and tested, living-learning community BPM, there is now a more inspiring framework for colleges and universities to use to improve their LLCs. By applying a typology of practice, it is possible to move LLCs from the basic level of implementation to more advanced levels of practice that optimally reinforce and enhance each portion of the model. Congratulations to the authors for providing the field a rock-solid model for advancing and improving LLCs. My goal in this *Afterword* is to amplify findings and add to their best practices framework, and to enthusiastically encourage expansion of LLCs in college and universities.

AMPLIFYING WHAT MATTERS FOR EFFECTIVE LLCS

Students involved in LLCs and other HIPs generally enjoy higher levels of learning and success. The positive benefits to students, especially those from identity groups historically and contemporarily underserved by higher education, strong interest by faculty, and endorsement from employers, have helped advance HIP adoption. Yet, in the rush to expand implementation, we must remember that the benefits from HIPs are only "when done well." Although the LLC Best Practice Model follows this admonition by specifying the integrated layers for effective LLCs, I believe it is important to remind LLC enthusiasts of the eight conditions that must be done well. As Kuh et al. (2013) commend, an experience labeled "high-impact" must:

- set appropriately high expectations for performance
- require a significant investment of time and effort
- facilitate substantive interactions with faculty and peers
- expose students to diverse perspectives and people
- offer frequent, timely, and constructive feedback
- structure opportunities for reflection and integrative learning

AFTERWORD

- remain relevant and have real-world application
- require students to demonstrate competence

Considering the revised BPM, I submit that the eight conditions could be examined as more explicit aims in the pyramid by LLC practitioners intent on implementing the model. The conditions are clearly part of the infrastructure, climate, and the intellectual and social experience. For example, academically and socially supportive climates in LLCs should intentionally facilitate interactions among students and faculty, while the intellectual and social experience layer must prioritize opportunities to expose students to diverse perspectives and people and structure opportunities for reflection and integration. The pyramid provides a more integrated framework for LLC practitioners to consider the conditions at these layers of the model and explore their explication at the foundational, intermediate, and advanced levels.

A few examples of what these practices look like in the design and activities of the LLC might help further illustrate the contribution of the HIP quality elements to the BPM. For instance, to ensure students exposure to diverse perspectives and people, LLCs could feature a service-learning assignment wherein students work in a setting populated by people from different backgrounds and demographics, such as an emergency housing shelter, which is coupled with residence hall or class discussions and journaling about the connections between readings and the service experience. Some LLC exemplars are featured in this book, including the Ashby College at the University of North Carolina Greensboro, which links its courses and cocurricular activities through a social justice curriculum, and the Engineering LLC at California Polytechnic University, which affiliates with Habitat for Humanity as its community partner to focus attention on local stakeholders and issues. Opportunities for structured reflection and integrated learning could also be enhanced through linked courses in a learning community, wherein one course instructor designs assignments that require students to draw on material covered in the other linked course or that connects to activities planned for the residential setting, and supplemented by a peer mentor who coordinates discussions at these events. Attending to these HIP conditions with intentionality in LLC design and implementation would help extend the layers and levels of the BPM.

Even more, HIP conditions are directly relevant to the assessment dimensions of the model. The conditions are outlined plainly in Ashley Finley's (2019) comprehensive approach to assessment, which is discussed in Chapter 7. The logic model to produce a comprehensive assessment plan for LLCs includes the conditions as outputs, or the processes and activities that the program undertakes to achieve their outcomes. The assessment of LLCs should take into account the extent to which these HIP conditions are present.

AFTERWORD

To further strengthen my argument to attend to the conditions for quality in LLCs, I'll highlight research conducted as part of the National Survey of Student Engagement's (NSSE's) ongoing effort to dig deeper into the qualities that make HIPs effective. In a comprehensive report examining students' exposure to high levels of HIP conditions (Kinzie et al., 2020), my colleagues and I found that students in learning communities (our research focused on learning communities broadly, not exclusively LLCs) were generally exposed to the eight quality dimensions in patterns consistent with what learning communities emphasize. For example, more than three quarters of students in learning communities indicated that they frequently worked with other students in their learning community and that this interaction substantially contributed to their learning. Almost the same proportion (71%) reported frequent levels of discussion and reflection in organized settings including inside and outside the learning community and 63% indicated that through their learning community they learned something that changed the way they understand an issue or concept. Students identified their learning community peers as the most likely source of frequent feedback. These are experiences and outcomes worth showcasing as evidence of high levels of quality in learning communities.

Our research also revealed the expected HIP conditions that were less prominent. For example, less than half (44%) of students in learning communities frequently interacted with faculty in their learning community and students also indicated low levels of exposure to experiences that helped them engage across difference. Students' open-ended comments suggested that while they appreciated "being able to lean on other students and become familiar with faculty," this interaction was usually shallow. Similarly, exchanging ideas and thoughts with people from other backgrounds was mentioned as a satisfying aspect of the learning community, yet the frequency of these interactions was low. These disappointing findings about conditions for quality are firmly based in the quality of relationships among students, faculty, and staff. The results give me great pause as I reflected on the conclusion from Felten and Lambert (2020) that relationships, including single, well-timed conversations and deeper life interactions, make for an excellent and transformative undergraduate education. Learning communities seem to be a fertile site for connecting with peers and faculty and staff, yet this does not seem to be currently optimized. Although our findings are inclusive of all types of learning communities – LLCs and connected courses without a residential component – I believe the implications are particularly actionable in LLCs. LLCs are perhaps best positioned to optimize the connections between teaching, learning, and living in ways that most enable relationship-based education. Infusing this feature and the conditions for substantive interaction with faculty and peers more explicitly in the BPM and assuring they are enhanced in LLC practice are vital.

EMPHASIZING EQUITY IN THE FRAMEWORK

The quality of LLCs cannot be enhanced without attention to equity. As the authors rightly point out, equal student access to beneficial practices like learning communities must be assured and LLCs should be assessed for the extent to which they welcome and support all students and produce equitable educational benefits. Strong social connections and supportive environments that LLCs do so well are associated with historically underrepresented and racially marginalized students' success. However, to assure this outcome, it is essential to design great educational experiences with equity in mind from the ground up. Heeding the words of Finley et al. (2022), "the imperative for equity in design is just as important as seeking equity in outcomes" (p. 27). Equity must be woven into the framework for LLCs to work.

LLCs with the explicit goal to engage and support students historically underrepresented in higher education are particularly noteworthy as we envision more inclusive colleges and universities. One example is the Key Communities at Colorado State University, which have long honored the identities and strengths of students in their learning communities that foster equity for students who are first generation to college, racially minoritized, and/or Pell-eligible. Key is an intentionally designed community of learners that offers individualized holistic support in a culture validating diverse student identities. Although the evidence of the impact of Key in the elimination of equity gaps in student persistence and the positive finding that it affords an inclusive and responsive space for students to thrive is robust, Novak et al. (2022) describe how they continue to interrogate equity in their offerings and are striving to reframe their learning community assessment to include more direct measures of student learning gains and qualitative inquiry to better understand the quality of the experience from a student-centered perspective.

As an educational program that centers on the educational benefit of community, LLCs are well positioned to insert equity into the design and assessment process. As learning community leaders design and assess their efforts using the BPM, I urge greater consideration of equity-minded lenses and frames that could make learning communities more equitable and affirming spaces for all students.

ENCOURAGING THE EXPANSION OF LLCS

At a time when public opinion polls are again doubting the value of a college degree and questioning the cost of a residential college experience, it is important for higher education to clearly convey its value. Part of this messaging is to persuasively communicate the quality and impact of educational experiences like HIPs that engage students deeply, are personally transformative, and are understood and valued by employers and other stakeholders. HIPs are educational

AFTERWORD

experiences that stand out in an undergraduate education, and most parents, siblings, employers, and even some legislators — particularly those who have participated in them — could identify them as educationally beneficial and worth providing to more students. We should promote their educational value and ensure they are accessible, affordable, and equitable for all students.

The expansion of LLCs can also be advanced through a greater focus on the synergies among HIPs and on the partnership between student and academic affairs. Today's student success agenda is even more dependent on linking practices like first-year seminars with living-learning communities, or scaffolding research skills in a STEM-themed learning community that serves as a foundation for later more mentored student-faculty research experiences. These linkages are dependent on campus-wide appreciation for experiential learning and HIPs, and stronger relationships among all campus educators. LLCs can be beacons of the most authentic student and academic affairs integration and more of this is needed.

Finally, as we reinvest in the community and social interactions disrupted during the pandemic and commit to creating more socially just educational systems, we must focus on campus experiences that help students and multiple stakeholders — faculty, staff, and administrators — who live in and build the campus community. As we endeavor to create more inclusive and effective LLCs, I am reminded of educator and social activist Parker Palmer, whose contemplations deeply influenced my early work in residential learning communities. His conclusion that community is not something to be built, but rather it must be present in the individual as a "capacity for connectedness" and cultivated through recognition of the comfort, encouragement, and support provided by others that we all need to be successful. LLCs are important sites for cultivating a capacity for connectedness.

The BPM provides a blueprint for addressing the sometimes mistaken impression that just putting a cohort of students together in learning communities will guarantee educational benefits. If you're after a supportive environment for engaging, deep, collaborative, and transformative learning that attracts students and invests talented faculty, then an LLC designed with the revised BPM and advanced typologies is your guide.

LLCs provide a tremendous opportunity to cultivate authentic connections in an integrated and educationally structured opportunity to learn with and support others. When done well, they can promote the exact type of faculty and student engagement we know delivers deep learning and fosters student success.

Jillian Kinzie
Associate Director, National Survey of Student Engagement
Center for Postsecondary Research
Indiana University Bloomington

REFERENCES

Dunn, M. S., & Dean, L. A. (2013). Together we can live and learn: Living-learning communities as integrated curricular experiences. *SCHOLE: A Journal of Leisure Studies and Recreation Education, 28*(1), 11–23.

Felten, P., & Lambert, L. M. (2020). *Relationship-rich education: How human connections drive success in college.* Baltimore, MD: Johns Hopkins University Press.

Finley, A. (2019). A comprehensive approach to assessment of high-impact practices (Occasional Paper No. 41). National Institute for Learning Outcomes Assessment.

Finley, A., McNair, T., & Clayton-Pedersen, A. (2022). Designing equity-centered high-impact practices. In J. Zilvinskis, J. Kinzie, J. Daday, K. O'Donnell & C. Vande Zande (Eds.), *Delivering on the promise of high-impact practices: Research and models for achieving equity, fidelity, impact, and scale* (pp. 17–29). Sterling, VA: Stylus.

Inkelas, K. K., Jessup-Anger, J. E., Benjamin, M., & Wawrzynski, M. R. (2018). *Living-learning communities that work: A research-based model for design, delivery, and assessment.* Sterling, VA: Stylus.

Inkelas, K. K., & Soldner, M. (2011). Undergraduate living–learning programs and student outcomes. In J. C. Smart & M. B. Paulsen (Eds.), *Higher education: Handbook of theory and research* (Vol. 26, pp. 1–55). New York: Springer.

Kinzie, J., McCormick, A. C., Gonyea, R. M., Dugan, B., & Silberstein, S. (2020, July). *Assessing quality and equity in high-impact practices: Comprehensive report.* Bloomington: Indiana University Center for Postsecondary Research.

Kuh, G. D., O'Donnell, K., & Reed, S. (2013). *Ensuring quality and taking high-impact practices to scale.* Washington, DC: Association of American Colleges and Universities.

Mayhew, M. J., Rockenbach, A. N., Bowman, N. A., Seifert, T. A., Wolniak, G. C., Pascarella, E. T., & Terenzini, P. T. (2016). *How college affects students: 21st century evidence that higher education works* (Vol. 3). San Francisco, CA: Jossey-Bass.

Novak, H., Nosaka, T., & Barone, R. (2022). Intentionally designing learning communities to advance authentic access and equity. In J. Zilvinskis, J. Kinzie, J. Daday, K. O'Donnell & C. Vande Zande (Ed.), *Delivering on the promise of high-impact practices: Research and models for achieving equity, fidelity, impact, and scale* (pp. 62–75). Sterling, VA: Stylus.

Strayhorn, T. L. (2023). Estimating differences in the effects of living–learning community participation on black students' sense of belonging at predominantly white and historically black colleges and universities. *Journal of College Student Development, 64*(2), 225–230.

The Association of College & University Housing Officers – International (ACUHO-I) is a professional association that strives to be the preeminent resource and champion for the global campus housing profession. Founded in 1952 and home to more than 17,000 professionals, ACUHO-I cultivates a diverse, inclusive, and equitable profession that delivers transformative residential student experiences. We do so through extensive knowledge resources, innovative operational models, courageous advocacy, and resolute community connections. ACUHO-I and its members are shaping the future of the campus housing profession.

With credible benchmarking data, research, and reports, ACUHO-I demonstrates the positive impact that campus housing and residence life have on student recruitment, retention, growth, and achievement. ACUHO-I helps campus housing departments elevate their profile, prioritize their needs, and inform the decisions that boost the reputation of their entire organization.

ACUHO-I offers educational resources, research products, leadership tools, and training programs that housing departments rely on to persuade influencers, improve performance, and produce exceptional campus housing and residence life solutions. Among the opportunities available to all members are an informative magazine, academic journal, content-rich conferences, focused institutes, online courses, a robust online community, and more, all geared to support, challenge, and inspire our members to greatness while serving their students with humility and care.

Index

academic 102; academic advising 30, 86; academic affairs administration 31, 32; academic affairs leadership 87, 97; academically engaged 43, 45, 51, 52, 55, 58; academic climate 40, 41, 43, 47; academic personnel 27; academic programming 3, 60, 100; academic programs 2, 3, 43; academic-residential partnerships 28
access 20, 86, 110, 119; access and equity 121; access programs 86
adequate resources: in original Best Practices Model 3, 5, 11, 14, 17; in revised Best Practices Model 18, 35, 55
advisory 29, 30, 66, 67, 103
advocacy 56, 58, 59, 62, 89, 122
alumni 10, 20, 40, 69, 74, 87
assessment: assessing academic climates 54; assessing LLC effectiveness 85; assessing student participation 82; assessment plans 86–88, 91, 94, 108; assessment types 82, 84
assignments 19, 20, 27, 37, 96, 117
attendance 82, 84

barriers 21, 51, 106, 110
benchmarking 83, 85, 86, 122
branding 20, 22, 23, 49, 100
budget 27, 30, 32–35, 38, 67

CA/community assistants/community advisors 25, 60, 68, 69
calendar 20, 97, 101
campus leaders 6, 10, 12, 13, 16, 81
capstone 58, 62, 92, 108, 109
career workshops 4, 7, 15, 60
celebrations 15, 71
champions 11, 15, 57, 89, 103, 122
cocurricular: cocurricular activities 4, 15, 30, 43, 70, 117; cocurricular environment 4, 6; cocurricular programming 6, 31
collaboration 3, 5, 22, 24, 25, 28, 100
community outreach 15, 66, 72, 73, 88–90
compensation 26, 31
coordinator 21, 24, 31, 69
courses for credit 16, 41, 58; critique of original Best Practices model 10, 14; in original Best Practices Model 4, 6
COVID-19 1, 7–9, 61, 110–114, 116
crisis 111, 112
curriculum 24, 29, 58, 92, 97, 105; curricular 96, 105, 115

dining 6, 18, 23, 46
diversity 2, 65, 70, 91, 100; diverse living environment 51; diverse perspectives 56, 85, 116, 117; diverse social identities 47; diverse student identities 119; diverse student population 115

INDEX

engineering 24, 44, 72, 117
equity 69, 99, 109, 119
expectations 28, 29, 56, 103; expectation of engagement 43, 44; high expectations 57, 116; job expectations 99
expenses 32–34, 38

facilities 18, 61, 69, 70, 84, 86
families 7, 21, 36, 50, 95
financial resources 3, 11
first-generation students 65, 110
first-year: first-year experience 58, 110; first-year seminars 30, 57, 120; first-year students 4, 60, 65, 70, 110; first-year students programming 43, 46
fundraising 34

government 29, 33, 67
graduation 67, 81, 85, 89, 92

High Impact Practice 1, 5, 11, 108
holiday 15, 72

identity(ies) 18–20, 47, 49, 53, 70, 71, 116, 119
institutional leaders 10, 85, 87, 94
intellectual experience 14, 15, 55–62, 68, 70
interdisciplinary 35, 56
internships 7, 60, 63, 92, 108

justice 29, 39, 43, 44, 63, 117

leadership positions 11, 26, 59, 67
learning outcomes 24, 35, 78, 83, 85, 87
LLC personnel 61, 73
logic model 85, 88–91, 94, 107–109, 117
lounge 20–22, 26

major 2, 25, 47, 60, 69, 80; major/career activities 15, 60, 89
marginalized 49, 51, 65
marketing 58, 92, 100, 102, 106

mattering 49, 50, 53, 54
mentors 15, 34, 45, 57, 62, 91; mentoring 4, 59, 67
minoritized 109, 113, 119

National Study of Living-Learning 4, 40
National Survey of Student Engagement 87, 92

outreach 4, 15, 29, 110, 111

parallel partnerships 68, 96, 105
partners 44, 61, 63, 96; partnership 10, 29, 37, 72, 100
peer 1, 4, 7, 62, 74, 93; peer influence 41, 42; peer interactions 2, 11, 41, 65, 89; peer leaders 11, 26, 34, 65; peer mentors 26, 37, 58–63, 68–71, 110; peer mentors example 22, 27, 34; peer mentors role 15, 74; peer staff 26, 70; peer support 15, 46, 60, 66, 68–70, 88–90; peer tutors 26, 60
personnel 89; in original Best Practices Model 13; in revised Best Practices Model 23, 35, 36, 55
physical space 89; in original Best Practices Model 13; in revised Best Practices Model 18, 20, 23, 36, 55

RA/resident assistant: critique of original Best Practices Model 11, 15; in revised Best Practices Model 23, 25, 26, 37; in social experience 59, 65–69, 74
recruitment 10, 58, 59, 62, 83, 98
remuneration 26, 31
representatives 29, 93, 103
Residence Life & Housing personnel 28
retention 65, 67, 85, 89, 90, 110; retention, first-year 49, 81
retreats 43, 66, 71

scholars 21, 45, 109
seminars 6, 23, 30, 31, 57, 120
sense of belonging 48, 49, 51, 53, 65, 93

sense of community 20, 65, 71, 72
service 4, 61, 67, 71, 72, 75
service learning 14, 86, 96, 109, 110, 117
social climate 90; critique of original Best Practices Model 4, 14; part of LLC climate 40, 41, 47, 48, 50
social experience 88, 117; critique of original Best Practices Model 11, 14, 15; in revised Best Practices Model 59, 65–68, 71–73
social justice 43, 44, 117
staffing 7, 24, 65, 73, 82
stakeholders 44, 100; in assessment 78, 87, 89; critique of original Best Practices model 12, 16
Student Affairs personnel 29
students: student engagement 14, 108, 115; student government 29, 33; student influencers 99; student leadership 66, 67, 88, 89; student outcomes 15, 77, 79, 81, 90, 91; student staff 26, 33, 37, 38, 69; student success ix, 1, 80, 115, 116, 120
study groups 7, 41, 50, 59–61
swag 49, 71
syllabi 61, 96, 97

technology 111
theme-aligned activities 74
traditions 15, 44, 70, 71, 75, 90
transition 35, 46, 115; transition to college 26, 55, 109
trust 30, 49, 50, 53, 100
tutoring 6, 26, 37, 60, 61, 63, 72

underrepresented 54, 65, 93, 114, 119

websites 8, 22, 23, 39, 92, 98

Made in the USA
Monee, IL
03 May 2026

49437770R00077